THE CHESHIRE CYCLEV

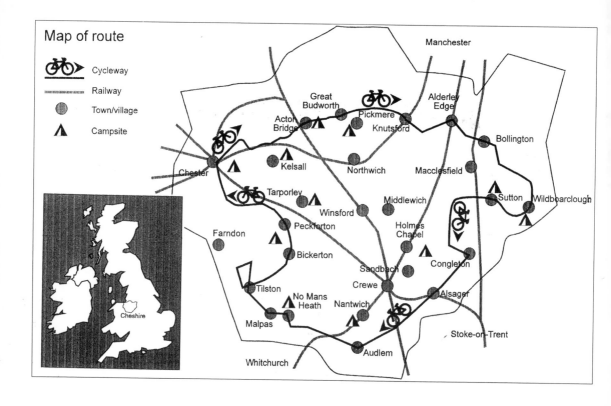

THE CHESHIRE CYCLEWAY

by

Alec and Val Scaresbrook

CICERONE PRESS
MILNTHORPE, CUMBRIA

© Alec and Val Scaresbrook, 1996
ISBN 1 85284 204 0
A catalogue record for this book is available from the British
Library

Front Cover: Cycling toward Sutton Lane Ends, stage 10
Photo: John Nuttall

CONTENTS

PREFACE

Anyone who's able to ride a bicycle can enjoy the Cheshire Cycleway. Whether a beginner or experienced cyclist, alone or in a group, young or old, just choose a cycle to suit your abilities and settle into a pace that allows you to enjoy the scenery.

Cheshire is a delightful county with a predominance of dairy farms providing an emerald setting for the black and white houses which are found scattered throughout the countryside and huddled together in the centres of towns and villages. Pubs, churches, railings, signposts and even the cattle grazing in the fields echo the monochrome scheme.

The Cheshire Cycleway takes you along quiet lanes to visit some of its gems on a 135 mile round trip which touches on Chester, takes you across the Cheshire plain and delivers fine views from high up in the gritstone hills, beautiful enough to be included in the Peak National Park.

The route makes an ideal basis for a week or two-week holiday, staying at each stop for several days to enable you to explore the immediate area. Many places of interest are free, although houses and gardens open to the public do make a charge, and a donation is appreciated by those struggling to keep their elderly churches in good repair.

Advice to Readers

Readers are advised that whilst every effort is taken by the author to ensure the accuracy of this guidebook, changes can occur which may affect the contents. It is advisable to check locally on transport, accommodation, shops etc but even rights-of-way can be altered.

The publisher would welcome notes of any such changes

PART ONE

Introduction

History of the Cheshire Cycleway

The idea of a cycleway was proposed by the Countryside and Recreation Department of Cheshire County Council with the aim of promoting recreation for residents of the county. The department worked with the local branch of the Cyclists' Touring Club, who made route suggestions, and the Cheshire Cycleway was launched in 1984. The engineering services of the county council arranged the signposting, and volunteers from the Cyclists' Touring Club check that the signs are still in place and pointing in the right direction.

A recent proposal is to create the Cheshire Cycleway Challenge, where gold, silver and bronze certificates will be awarded to those completing the cycleway within a certain time. Contact the county council for details.

How to use this guide

The Cheshire Cycleway is signposted in a clockwise direction, so our guide also takes you clockwise around the county.

The signs show the standard cycle route symbol of a white cycle on a blue background. Unfortunately the signs don't generally merit their own post, so are mounted on the nearest convenient road sign - not always in the most suitable position for a cyclist to spot. The signs are not in the same place at every junction so you have to develop a sixth sense for little blue signs hidden in the hedgerow. And, of course, the sign may have gone missing or have been twisted around since the last inspection by the eagle-eyed cycling club volunteers.

This is where the guide will help you, pointing out landmarks on the route and confirming that you are still heading in the right direction.

We've split the route into stages, each with a map, approximate distances, directions and information about places along the way, or close by. We suggest that you study each map and read through the directions before you start each stage, so that landmarks will jog your memory and you needn't keep stopping to scrutinise the map.

We've placed some directions within asterisks (*) to indicate where you should leave the route to visit a nearby place of interest, or take avoiding action when faced with busy main roads or steep hills. Unfortunately some of these obstacles are unavoidable unless you take a very tortuous route, which we've left to you to devise.

You don't need maps to follow the cycleway, but if you're like us and want to get your bearings, then you'll be happier with maps in your bicycle bag. The Ordnance Survey 1:50,000 Landranger maps nos. 117 and 118 cover most of the county and enable you to plan off-route excursions to see things that you're particularly interested in. The OS maps are also handy if you need to go off-route to find a phone box, railway station or large town.

What is the route like?

Most of Cheshire consists of an undulating plain, varying in height between 49ft (15m) and 298ft (91m) above sea level. This low-lying plain is covered in sands, gravels and clays, deposited after the last ice age. The clay provides rich farmland and is the reason for such a strong dairy farming industry here. The sandier soils are exploited by horticultural growers, and the pure sands and gravels are excavated by the mineral companies, leaving large water-filled pits in their wake. Smaller pools have formed in old marl pits, a legacy from the past, when marl (clay) was dug out and spread on the land to improve its productivity.

Despite Cheshire being mainly low-level, it's not all cycling on the flat. The county is criss-crossed with canals, providing picturesque picnic places and pub stops, plus plenty of exercise surmounting the steeply humpbacked bridges. The plain is also interrupted by a north-south ridge of sandstone and further east there's a shorter escarpment with its steep face on the north-east side. The cycleway crosses both of these ridges, giving you a foretaste of sterner hills to come on the eastern edge of the county, where the route climbs to 1234ft (376m) above sea level. Here, land was pushed upwards along the line of the Red Rock Fault, exposing the surface layers to erosion until the hard millstone grits were reached. The contrast with the plain is marked. These gritstone hills and moors provide a different environment, with the extra height above sea level creating a harsh climate. Houses are huddled in the valleys, although farmhouses brave the slopes, tucked into hollows to escape the wind and snow. There are sheep in the fields instead of cattle, and the stock are kept in by stone walls, not hedgerows. You can even hear the difference - the joyful sounds of songbirds on the plain are replaced by the mournful calls of curlew and golden plover.

How long will it take?

If you're a keen and fit cyclist, then you'll already know what sort of distance you can cover in a day. But it's difficult to say how far ordinary mortals will cover. We tackled the route in a leisurely fashion and took five days overall, taking longer to cover the stages in the eastern hills, where there are some leg-aching sections.

There's no point in rushing for the sake of it, since there are so many places to visit that are just off the route. Much better to cycle the route one day, and spend the next on sight-seeing. If you want a break from cycling, there's the option of bus, train or taxi to take you to your chosen destination.

Planning the stages

It's possible to divide the route into stages according to the position of campsites, bed and breakfast accommodation, or both.

Tourist information centres offer a comprehensive accommodation information and booking service.

Farmhouses offering bed and breakfast abound in Cheshire and there are small hotels in most towns. The tourist information centres also keep a list of campsites, but we've found that these tend to be sketchy. Membership of the Camping & Caravanning Club comes in handy here, because the club supplies a comprehensive list of sites and their facilities. For peace of mind, book ahead at busy times, although most campsite owners will squeeze a cyclist or two into a corner on a busy weekend. Just check that you aren't required to provide your own sanitation. After all, it's tricky to fit a Porta-pottie and toilet tent on a bike.

If you've set your heart on visiting a particular place of interest, we can't emphasise enough that you should check the opening dates, days and times with the local tourist information centre or the place itself. This also applies to cafes and restaurants. Because details change from year to year, we've listed relevant addresses and phone numbers for each stage.

There are plenty of pubs along the route which serve meals, although not all pubs serve food at all times. There's usually at least one cafe in each town that's passed and many of the houses and gardens open to the public have tea rooms. We also found some small shops which made up filled rolls and sandwiches, but this service could change.

Shopping for supplies shouldn't be a problem, with supermarkets in the towns open daily. Some village shops along the cycleway still observe an early closing day (usually Wednesday or Thursday), but you're always within cycling distance of a town. We've found post offices to be very informative on the subject of shops and opening hours if the tourist information centre can't help. Find the post office phone numbers in the *Yellow Pages* (Freephone 0800 600 900).

Short cuts

If you can't face the hilly stages, or need to take a short cut to a campsite or town, don't ignore the potential of canal towpaths and trains.

Canal towpaths

You'll need a cycling permit (free) to use these, obtainable from any local office of the British Waterways Board (look in the phone book). The only drawback to towpath cycling is other people. The towpaths are usually narrow, and popular with families for a stroll at weekends, so be prepared to make slow progress. And if there's a fishing match on, be prepared to make no progress at all. The fishing season runs from mid-June to mid-March, and competitions tend to be at the weekend. Canal fishermen now use very long rods which inevitably obstruct the path and when a match is on you could meet fifty fishermen spaced evenly along the canal bank.

Trains

Currently there are a number of towns and villages on or close to the cycleway that are served by train, some more frequently than others. Stations between Chester and Manchester are particularly well served at present. But don't rely on there being a train; check first. At present, most trains carry cycles, but the situation could change, so contact British Rail in Manchester (Tel: 0161 832 8353) for the latest situation.

What sort of bicycle?

The type of cycle doesn't really matter, as long as it is the right size for you and has the right equipment fitted to it. You can obtain good advice from specialist cycling shops, where staff can ensure that you have sufficient gears to tackle the hills and travel efficiently over flat sections. You'll need reflectors and lights for safety on dull days and at night, plus mudguards for comfort. These prevent a spray of water, mud and worse being thrown up by the tyres over you and anyone behind you. Full mudguards are fitted to touring bikes as standard, but are not often seen on mountain bikes. However, there are suitable mudguards available to fit mountain bikes.

Your cycle must also be able to take whatever luggage you'll have. If you send on your bags by taxi, you'll only need to carry a few items in a handlebar bag or a specially designed mountain cycling rucksack (ordinary rucksacks are unsuitable for cycling). If camping, you'll need a complete set of pannier bags to carry all the gear. Take your bike with you when shopping for a pannier rack - not all racks fit all bikes.

Bicycle hire

Even if you own a cycle, it may be more convenient to hire one locally instead of transporting it by train or car.

Hire facilities come and go, so for up-to-date information you need to consult the relevant *Yellow Pages* (public libraries stock the whole set). At the time of writing there are three cycle hire services close to the cycleway:

Davies Bros (Cycles) Ltd, 6-8 Cuppin St, Chester, Cheshire, tel: 01244 319204/318899

Groundwork Trust, Discovery Centre, Grimshaw Lane, Bollington, Nr Macclesfield, Cheshire SK10 5JB, tel: 01625 572681

South Cheshire Cycle Hire, Meadow View Farm, Crewe Lane South, Farndon, Cheshire, tel: 01829 271242

What to wear

You needn't splash out on a full set of specialist cycle clothing, but you do need to choose your clothes with comfort, safety and the weather in mind. If you already have walking clothing then you'll be well equipped. If not, spend a while browsing around a shop which caters for those indulging in outdoor activities. You'll find plenty of general outdoor clothing on offer here, including budget garments from companies such as Regatta (see cover photograph). Cycling and mountaineering shops sell specialist mountain cycle clothing from companies such as Karrimor and Ronhill.

The most comfortable legwear is that made from stretchy material. Leggings or track suit trousers with narrow hems (no need for cycle clips) are ideal. For warmer weather, many cyclists prefer shorts. However, you may regret this choice when you have to squeeze over into the nettles and brambles to allow an oncoming vehicle to pass you on a narrow lane.

For tops, think in layers. You get very hot cycling uphill or against the wind, and chill off quickly when freewheeling downhill. Modern fabrics used in outdoor clothing include fleece, which is warm and lightweight, and although not waterproof, dries off very quickly after rain. Some fleece garments are designed to be windproof, but most let the wind through.

The most suitable fabric to wear beneath fleece is a garment made of artificial fibres which can wick your perspiration away from your skin. But don't worry, a cotton T-shirt or long-sleeved shirt will do if your budget doesn't stretch to specialist base-layers.

Waterproofs are essential - a jacket plus overtrousers are more practical than a cape and can be used elsewhere, not just on the bike. Breathable fabrics prevent that unpleasant build-up of cold clammy wetness and have the added advantage of being excellent windproofs on dry days.

Most footwear is suitable, but do avoid very soft-soled sandals - rigid soles make pedalling easier.

A pair of gloves is handy for windy days and downhill runs on cool days. Ordinary gloves are suitable, but special cycling gloves, which are padded, help protect your hands from vibrations and pressure if you're using drop handlebars.

There's nothing worse than getting something in your eye when cycling along. Prevent dust, grit and flies from causing problems by wearing wrap-round cycling glasses. There are dark ones for bright sunny days and clear versions for dull days.

Helmets are now widely available, and of course protect the skull, but that's not always the bit which comes into contact with the road or another vehicle. If you decide to equip yourself or your family with helmets, follow the instructions and make sure that the helmet sits squarely on the top of the head, with the chinstrap pulled tight. Helmets perched loosely on the back of the wearer's head offer little protection.

And last, but not least, whatever you wear, ensure that it cannot become entangled in the chain, spokes, levers and other fittings. You wouldn't believe how easy it is for cords dangling from clothing (and long laces swinging over shoes) to become caught up in the workings of a cycle, tangling you in the machine at a crucial moment.

What to take

Cycle bags and cyclists' rucksacks are widely available in the specialist shops and by mail order. Well-known British makes include Carradice and Karrimor; imported makes include Jack Wolfskin, Ortlieb and VauDe. A handlebar bag with clear map case on the lid is very useful, doubling up as a shoulder bag for valuables when leaving the bike. Most bags and rucksacks are stitched and inevitably leak, so pack everything that must stay dry in strong plastic bags. Alternatively, choose bags without stitched seams and with roll-down tops, to ensure complete water-proofness.

Apart from your personal kit, plus camping and cooking equipment if appropriate, there's the cycling equipment to carry.

A good cycle lock is essential. Otherwise you could come back from sight-seeing or shopping to find that you've no transport. If possible, lock the bike to an immovable object, but take care not to inconvenience or obstruct passers-by.

A puncture repair kit, tyre levers and pump are also essential (find out before the trip how to fix a puncture). If you're an adept cycle mechanic, then you won't need to be told what other tools and spares to take. Most of us have to rely on the cycle shop for all but minor problems though, so we've listed shops offering spares and repairs on (or close to) the cycleway. As ever, check in the *Yellow Pages* and *Thomson's Directory* for up-to-date details, and check opening days and hours.

In addition to a first aid kit for the bike, make up one for yourself to cater for minor problems such as cuts, grazes, insect bites and headaches. If you're lucky with the weather, you'll need suntan lotion and if you're unlucky with insects, you'll need repellent too.

Cycling techniques

A smooth cycling rhythm is worth mastering for energy-saving and comfortable progress. Once settled into your rhythm, you'll find that you travel in a stable and predictable path, which adds to your safety when sharing the tarmac with cars and lorries.

Aim for a constant pedalling speed, whatever the conditions, by using the gears to the full. With some fine tuning, you should move forward with the minimum of pedalling effort.

This technique works well on undulating roads and is far less tiring than pedalling furiously for a while, losing speed while coasting along to take a rest, and then frantically pedalling to pick up speed again.

It's also less tiring to be in the right gear on the approach to a steep section, rather than wait until you're on it before selecting the gear. Otherwise you can end up wobbling around, having lost your momentum, and will have to push hard on the pedals to keep moving forward until you've selected the right gear.

Avoid the back-wrenching bad habit of exaggerating shoulder movement when pushing down on each pedal. This sort of riding twists the cycle frame and puts stress on the wheels, especially if laden with pannier bags. The result is broken spokes - not a simple roadside repair. If you feel that you need to put your shoulder into it, you're in too high a gear. The answer is to use a lower gear or get fitter, or both.

Anticipating gear requirements takes some practice and if you are new to cycling, you may find that you are more preoccupied with route-finding and dodging the traffic than maintaining a steady rhythm. But you'll suddenly discover that it's become second nature and you no longer have to think about it.

Safe cycling

It's important to make yourself visible to other road users, because a cycle plus rider is such an insignificant object when compared with the bulk of a car or truck.

Make yourself visible from the front and back with bright clothing that shows up during the day, plus lights and reflectors that shine at night. Bright and reflective fabric strips are incorporated into pannier bags and specialist cycle clothing - belts, sashes and armbands can be worn over ordinary clothing too.

Reflectors fitted to the wheel spokes ensure that you are visible from the side at night.

Another very useful item to fit to the cycle is a plastic 'flag' which is hinged to fold flat against the cycle when not needed. In use, it projects by about a foot and has a noticeable effect on motorists, who give a much wider berth than usual.

A steady and predictable cycling rhythm aids safety because motorists can see your intended line of travel. Positive and decisive cycling is also important - if you have to turn right, look over your shoulder and if there's space between you and following traffic, give a clear arm signal and make the manoeuvre. Don't dither.

Turning right is hazardous because you have to cross the carriageway and hover on the centre line if there's oncoming traffic. The problem is that motorists may not register your presence. On busy roads, waiting on the left-hand side of the road until traffic has cleared is preferable to hanging around in the middle of the road.

Creeping along either side of a line of slow-moving or stationary vehicles is another unhealthy occupation. If you are a car driver then you'll know how infrequently you look over your left shoulder before turning left at a junction. The other danger comes from a passenger

14

suddenly deciding to get out while the car is temporarily stationary. An opening car door is quite an obstruction to your progress. A line of parked cars can also offer hazards if the vehicles contain drivers or passengers. Drivers are prone to nipping into a parking place and jumping out to pop into the nearest shop. Passengers, especially children, are even more likely to open the car door without looking. The last thing on their minds is a cyclist moving quickly and quietly towards them. Be ready to shout and brake hard - swerving could get you into a worse situation.

When in traffic queues or on roundabouts, position yourself in the centre of the lane so that motorists have a full view of you and aren't tempted to squeeze you into the kerb.

Finally, although cycling two abreast is permissible on the roads, it can cause aggravation to motorists, who then behave aggressively and recklessly. So don't block other road-users' progress for too long, for safety's sake.

White Lion Inn,
Barthomley.
(Stage 13)

PART TWO
Explanatory Notes

We've split up the cycleway route into 18 stages for ease of mapping. Each stage includes a map which shows road numbers where relevant, nearby railway stations, pubs along the route (but not in the towns and villages), cafes and campsites along or close to the route and detours to nearby places of interest.

The directions and descriptions include approximate distances and indicate the terrain encountered. Detours are indicated in the directions by an asterisk (*).

Symbols used on the maps

Cycleway	🚲▶	Railway station	O ≷
Detour	·········	Railway line	▬▬▬
A road	▬▬▬	Campsite	▲

Above:
Cyclists in Delamere Forest
(Stage 3)

Left:
Anderton boat lift
(Stage 4)

Left:
Autumn woodland, Alderley Edge *(Stage 7)*

Below:
Great Budworth *(Stage 5)*

Chester to Mickle Trafford (2½ miles)

The route skirts the eastern edge of the city, threads through housing, and takes you eastward, leaving the rush and tear of Chester behind and offering views of rolling farmland in the foreground, with the hump of Delamere Forest on its sandstone ridge in the distance. On the skyline to the left, the oil refinery chimneys of Ellesmere Port jar the eye.

If you're starting from Chester railway station, head for the A56 to Warrington in order to pick up the cycleway alongside the A41. If you're not keen on the main roads, use the Ordnance Survey map to find a way through the back streets. To avoid cycling through Chester altogether, take the train from Chester to Mouldsworth, picking up the cycleway at the beginning of Stage 3.

Tourist information

For up-to-date details of opening dates and times, admission charges and special events contact:
Chester Tourist Information Centre (TIC), Town Hall, Northgate St, Chester, Cheshire CH1 2HJ, tel: 01244 317962 or 318356.

Grosvenor Museum, Grosvenor St, Chester, Cheshire, tel: 01244 321616 (information on museum, city wall towers and heritage centre).

Dewa Roman Experience, Pierpoint Lane, off Bridge St, Chester, Cheshire CH1 2BJ, tel/fax: 01244 343407.

Chester

Chester is well furnished with shops, including cycling shops, and a range of eating and drinking establishments, from cafes and pubs to restaurants and hotels. Every day (except Sunday) is market day, so the streets are always busy with people and traffic. Guided tours are available and these are probably the best way to discover the delights of Chester in a limited time - enquire at the tourist information centre (TIC) for details. There's also a plethora of museums and lively displays from different periods of history, which you can find out about from the TIC.

For a summary of the history of the city from prehistoric times to the present day, visit Chester's Heritage Centre (admission charge).

The Grosvenor Museum (free admission) concentrates on life here in Roman times. Chester was the site of the largest Roman fortress in Britain and numerous items have been discovered over the years. These are now on imaginative display in the museum. If you're keen to learn more about life in Roman times, try the Dewa Roman Experience (admission charge), which envelops you in a re-creation of the past.

The city walls owe their existence to the Romans and are open to the public (free admission), giving good views of the centre and surroundings. Visit Bonewaldesthorne's tower (small admission charge) and walk along the connecting spur wall to the Water Tower. This was built in the early 14th century to guard the harbour of Chester, but you need imagination to visualise the days when seagoing vessels moored here - the river silted up long ago and the Water Tower is surrounded by dry land, now a public park. A camera obscura gives a panoramic view of the area.

King Charles' Tower (small admission charge), also on the city walls, contains a small English Civil War exhibition. Chester played an important part in the Civil War, with deep division amongst the inhabitants, even within families. At the end of 1644, Chester was besieged, holding out until February 1646, when the Parliamentarians finally took possession and Cheshire's part in the Civil War ceased.

On a lighter note, the city boasts the oldest racecourse in Britain (the Roodee, visible from the city walls), where racing dates from the mid-16th century. The city's rows are also famous - these are medieval rows of two-tier shops. The roofs of the shops at street level provide a walkway and frontage for the shops above. The walkways are covered and provide a good view of the streets below, and shelter from any rain too.

Amongst the many old buildings in Chester, the most important is the cathedral. Its stones span 900 years, including parts of the original abbey church of St Werburgh that somehow survived King Henry VIII's Dissolution of the Monasteries. Not all is old though; the newest addition is a bell-tower that was built in the grounds in 1975.

Food and drink
Chester centre.
Chester outskirts (shops may observe Wednesday early closing).

Stage 1

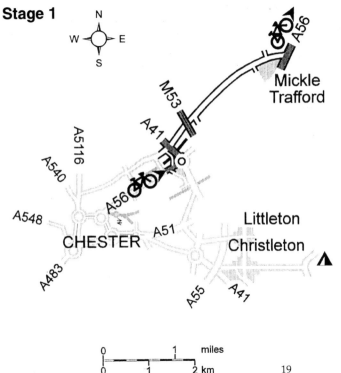

Directions

At roundabout junction of A56 and A41, turn left onto Greenfield Lane, which runs parallel to the A41.

Use cycle track to cross A41 at end of Greenfield Lane.

Left onto cycle track on pavement.

First right (into Mannings Lane).

Cycle to A56, skirting Mickle Trafford.

19

Campsites
None on route.
See Stage 18.

Cycle repairs/spares
The Cycle Centre, 19 Charles St, Hoole, Chester, Cheshire, tel: 01244 340420.
Davies Bros (Cycles) Ltd, 6-8 Cuppin St, Chester, Cheshire, tel: 01244 319204/318899.
Dave Miller Cycles, 41 Frodsham St, Chester, Cheshire, tel: 01244 326506.

Cycle hire
Davies Brothers (Cycles) Ltd - see above.

Nearest railway station
Chester (Chester - Manchester line).

This stage unfortunately follows a couple of miles of the very busy A56, but, if you're nervous of the traffic, it's possible to take the illegal but safer route on the pavement until it peters out at the railway bridge. If you do this, then you must give all consideration to pedestrians, although it's unlikely that you'll come across many.

Once off the main road, the route takes pleasantly quiet, tree-lined country lanes past Manley Mere and on to the village of Mouldsworth and its motor museum.

Cycling is mainly on the flat or downhill, with the exception of one notable 1 in 10 hill after passing under the railway bridge beyond Manley Mere. It's a third of a mile pull, fortunately surmounted by a post office/ store where you can rest, recover and reward yourself with sweets or cakes.

Tourist information

Chester TIC, Town Hall, Northgate St, Chester, Cheshire CH1 2HJ, tel: 01244 317962 or 318356.

Mouldsworth Motor Museum, Smithy Lane, Mouldsworth, Cheshire CH3 8AR, tel: 01928 731781. Sailsports Windsurfing Centre, Lower Farm, Manley, via Warrington, Cheshire WA6 0PE, tel: 01928 740243.

St Peter's church, Plemstall

Follow the lane beneath the railway line to discover this lonely church by the River Gowy. The church is said to owe its foundation to a fisherman washed ashore here; hence the name. On the left side of Plemstall Lane, close to the bridge, there's a spring called St Plegmund's Well, where tradition has it that the converted were baptised. The well was restored in the early 1900s. Plegmund was a cleric who lived here as a hermit in the second half of the 9th century. He was summoned to court by King Alfred the Great when he ascended the throne, to act as his tutor. Plegmund became Archbishop of Canterbury in 890 and when he died in 914 he was buried in the cathedral.

Mouldsworth Motor Museum (admission charge)
This is housed in a former waterworks treatment centre, itself of interest, built of concrete in art deco style in 1937. The display includes cars, motorcycles, cycles, early pedal cars, toys and a reconstruction of a 1920s garage.

Food and drink
Pubs along the route.
Coffee shop at the Sailsports Windsurfing Centre.
Post office/store in Manley.

Campsites
None on route.
See Stage 3.

Cycle spares/repairs
None on route.
See Stage 1.

Nearest railway station
Mouldsworth (Chester - Manchester line).

Directions

Left onto A56.

Detour first right to Plemstall church (¹/₂ mile)

Second right turning after railway bridge (signposted B5132, windsurfing centre).

Left at next crossroads (signposted windsurfing centre).

Left at T junction.

Immediately right at T junction into Manley Lane.

Left at T junction.

Detour right to Mouldsworth Motor Museum (¹/₂ mile)

Immediately right at T junction (into Station Rd).

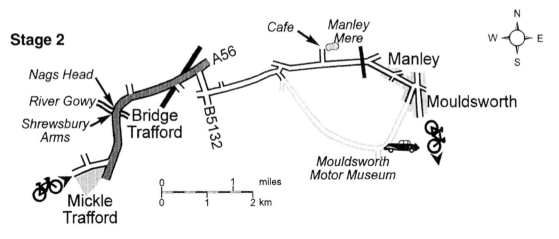

23

From Mouldsworth the route takes you downhill, only to send you climbing up again, to 266ft (81m) above sea level in Delamere Forest Park. The consolation is that the 1 in 20 hill only lasts for about half a mile. The Forest Park is managed for recreation as well as timber, and is not all conifers. The route is lined with beautiful broad-leaved trees providing pleasant shade in summer and delightful colours in autumn. The appropriately named switchback road is well supplied with laybys and picnic sites. If possible, plan your ride to avoid weekends, when there's a lot of traffic around. Once out of the trees, the route takes you through quiet villages and offers good views over the Cheshire countryside.

Tourist information

Chester TIC, Town Hall, Northgate St, Chester, Cheshire CH1 2HJ, tel: 01244 317962 or 318356.

Tourism Officer, Amenities and Recreation Dept, Vale Royal Borough Council, Wyvern House, The Drumber, Winsford, Cheshire, tel: 01606 862862.

Delamere Forest Park, Forest Enterprise, Linmere, Delamere, Northwich, Cheshire CW8 2JD, tel: 01606 882167.

Station House Cafe, Station Rd, Delamere, Northwich, Cheshire, tel: 01606 889825.

Delamere Forest

This area is a relic of an ancient forest called Mara, which was a Royal Forest by the 14th century. A forest was a protected hunting area, not necessarily a heavily wooded district. The red and fallow deer which roamed here were the property of the Crown, although it was usually the Crown's agents who did the hunting. Not all deer were killed; often they were given as breeding stock for newly created forests and deer parks elsewhere.

The area to the south of the present day woods, shown on the Ordnance Survey map as the Old Pale, marks the large enclosure (around 182 hectares (450 acres)) made in 1337 to hold deer. The deer population was wiped out during the Civil War and it wasn't considered feasible to restock afterwards because the

Directions

Downhill along Station Rd (B5393).

First left (signposted Delamere Forest).

Detour for campsite (2 miles)

Straight on at crossroads.

Straight on at crossroads in Hatchmere.

Detour left for pub and picnic site (350yds) or right for Delamere Station and cafe (1 mile), Linmere Forest Centre, WC (1 1/2 miles)

Right at fork (into Post Office Lane).

Right at T junction, into Norley.

Ignore first two left turns, close together.

Left at fork (into Maddocks Hill), opposite village hall.

Left at T junction into School Bank.

Continue for about 1 mile.

Pass Bent Lane on left.

Next left into Onston Lane.

Right at T junction onto B5153 (Station Rd).

Acton Bridge

The Maypole

Hazel Pear Inn

B5153

A49

Onston Lane

The Tiger's Head

Carriers Inn

B5152

Picnic site WC

Cafe

Delamere Forest

Norley

Hatchmere

Mouldsworth

The Goshawk

Brine's Brow picnic site

Picnic site WC

Linmere Visitor Centre WC

Cafe

N
W — E
S

0   1   miles
0   1   2 km

Left by Hazel Pear Inn.

Cycle to A49 (main road Whitchurch to Warrington)

25

woods had also been depleted and there was little shelter left for the animals. Replanting occurred much later, with oak and pine in the 19th century, and further plantings by the Forestry Commission earlier this century. The forest now covers 785 hectares (1940 acres) and is the largest block of established woodland in Cheshire. Because of the mixture of age and type of trees, there are diverse habitats here, which make the area important for all sorts of wildlife.

Delamere Forest Park (no charge)

The public have been coming here in droves, by train and car, for years, prompting the Forestry Commission to provide some self-guided trails in the forest, a small visitor centre and parking along the roads in 1969. Then in 1987 the area was designated as a Forest Park and consequently facilities for the public were improved, with a larger visitor centre plus shop, educational facilities and a ranger service. Now over 250,000 people visit the forest annually, although this doesn't prevent normal forestry operations continuing. There's also a tree nursery of 81 hectares (200 acres), where tree seedlings are nurtured for supply to other forests south of a line from Merseyside to the Humber. You can see the polythene tunnels and lines of seedlings from the track by the visitor centre.

The forest is criss-crossed with paths for pedestrians and routes for cyclists, including mountain cycling areas. There are free leaflets giving details of routes, including walks to view (from a distance) the iron age Eddisbury hill fort and see the long-disused Roman road that linked York and Chester. Apart from supplying leaflets, the Forest Centre has a small exhibition about Delamere and also sells books and maps.

Hazel Pear Inn, Acton Bridge

The unusual name of this pub refers to the hazel or hassle pear, which was grown in this area from the end of the 19th century. It is a particularly hardy pear, able to blossom and crop in the north, unlike so many pear varieties. The crop was sent by rail to Liverpool market in large quantities and was used not only for eating, but for dyeing. Apparently a yellow dye can be extracted from the skins and twigs, and it's said that fruit from this area was used in Liverpool to dye First World War uniforms a khaki colour. Most of the orchards were grubbed up from the 1960s onwards, to make way for housing.

Food and drink

Pubs along the route.

Cafes at Hatchmere (open daily except Tuesday) and Delamere Station (open daily).

Village shop in Norley (opposite the Tiger's Head) and Acton Bridge.

Campsites

2 miles off-route: Ignore turning to Delamere Forest, continue straight on to Ashton, turn left to Kelsall, left onto A54 to Northwich and look for campsite on right. Northwood Hall, Frodsham Street, Kelsall, Chester, Cheshire CW6 0RP, tel: 01829 752569.

WCs, hot showers, laundry facilities.

Also, site at Acton Bridge, see Stage 4.

Cycle spares/repairs

Hartford Cycles, 22 Greenbank Lane, Hartford (nr Northwich), Cheshire, tel: 01606 76170.

Jack Gee Cycles, 136-140 Witton St, Northwich, Cheshire, tel: 01606 43029.

Nearest railway station

Delamere Station (Chester - Manchester line).

Acton Bridge (Liverpool - Crewe line).

Acton Bridge to Great Budworth (5¹/₂ miles)

This stage follows the busy A49 for about half a mile, in order to cross the Weaver Navigation, before turning off onto much calmer (and narrower) lanes which give good views over north Cheshire. After crossing the Trent and Mersey Canal for the first time, there's about 200yds of a 1 in 13 hill to pedal up. Then the gradient slackens and level lanes lead to Little Leigh, with the surreal view of a golden weathercock perched on the tree tops ahead. Apart from crossing the A533, it's lanes all the way to Comberbach and Great Budworth, with the last section giving glimpses of the church tower ahead, and views to the right over Budworth Mere. This large mere may have been caused by natural salt subsidence. Mid-Cheshire has huge underground deposits of salt which have been extracted for centuries, but the only evidence of the industry on this stage is the Weaver Navigation and its swing bridge (painted black and white, of course).

Tourist information

Chester TIC, Town Hall, Northgate St, Chester, Cheshire CH1 2HJ, tel: 01244 317962 or 318356.

Tourism Officer, Amenities and Recreation Dept, Vale Royal Borough Council, Wyvern House, The Drumber, Winsford, Cheshire, tel: 01606 862862.

The Salt Museum, 162 London Rd, Northwich, Cheshire CW9 8AB, tel: 01606 41331.

The Lion Salt Works and Groundwork Discovery Centre, Marston, Northwich, Cheshire CW9 6ES, tel: 01606 41823.

Acton Swing Bridge

The River Weaver was canalised in the 18th century, linking Northwich and Winsford with the sea in order to improve the transport of salt. Before that, salt was moved by road to the nearest navigable part of the river, which is north of here at Frodsham. To begin with, sailing flats were used to move the salt, although they weren't sailed when on the river, but hauled by men on the banks. After a towpath was constructed, horses replaced the men. Once steam barges came into use, more headroom was needed beneath the road

Directions

Left onto A49.
Detour right for campsite (1/2 mile)
First right.
First right.
Left onto A533 (Northwich to Runcorn road).
Immediately right to Comberbach.
Right at T junction into Cogshall Lane.
Right at T junction in Comberbach.
Left at T junction.

Detour right for Marbury country park, WC (1 mile), Trent and Mersey Canal (1¼ miles), Anderton boat lift (1¼ miles) and Northwich Salt Museum (3¾ miles)
Right into Budworth Lane.

CARE - steep downhill section to main road (A559).
Detour right onto A559, first right at crossroads, to the Lion Salt Works, Groundwork Discovery Centre, WC (2 miles)

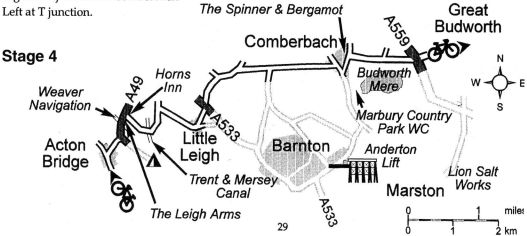

Stage 4

bridges, so these were replaced by ones which swung to one side to allow the boats to pass.

This bridge was built in 1932 and was the first in the country to rest on a floating pontoon. It replaced an older bridge which was sited a few hundred yards upstream. You can see the original abutments on the river banks from the Leigh Arms car park.

Trent and Mersey Canal

The Trent and Mersey Canal was completed in 1777 at the instigation of pottery manufacturers in Stoke-on-Trent to provide a safe method of transport for their finished products and also improve the movement of the bulk raw materials. The canal runs parallel to the Weaver Navigation for much of its route because the trustees of the Weaver Navigation would not contemplate links with the canal, for fear of losing trade to it. The canal forms part of the Cheshire Ring (a 67 mile circuit around the Bridgewater, Trent and Mersey, Macclesfield and Peak Forest canals), which is a popular holiday route.

The canal provides a useful route eastward to the Lion Salt Works if you prefer to avoid the alternative detour later via the A559.

Anderton Boat Lift (view from towpath)

The Anderton boat lift is unique in Britain and quite a sight, even in the semi-derelict state that it's in now. Find it by taking the road on your left once in Anderton village. Cross the canal footbridge, from where you'll have a good view of the top of the lift and the River Weaver below.

The need for a boat lift came about as a result of the Weaver Navigation trustees refusing to co-operate with the canal builders. Eventually, common sense prevailed and thought was put into the transfer of boats and their loads from one waterway to the other. These came closest together at Anderton, although there was the problem of a 50ft (15m) difference in levels.

The lift was developed to move barges and long boats between the river and canal in massive water tanks supported on hydraulic cylinders and pistons. The original lift was completed in 1875 and eliminated the need for cargoes to be manhandled. The lift was a great success, but the polluted canal water caused corrosion inside the cylinders and in 1906 the lift was rebuilt, over the top of the original structure and using part of it. The new lift used gears and pulleys instead of hydraulics and continued to be used by leisure traffic once commercial traffic ceased in the 1960s. But in 1982, structural faults were found and the lift had to be closed. It now rather forlornly awaits restoration.

Salt industry
The wich towns - Northwich, Leftwich, Middlewich and Nantwich - are salt towns. Romans were the first documented exploiters of the salt deposits beneath the Cheshire plain, and the mineral is still removed in vast amounts, but by methods which have eliminated the dramatic subsidence problems seen in the past. As a result of the subsidence, special timber-framed liftable buildings were designed and built in nearby Northwich, enabling hydraulic jacks to level any building affected by this problem. There are still 50 of these buildings in the town. Buildings in High St have been lifted up by over 20ft (6m) in total over the years. The Salt Museum (admission charge) explains every aspect of the industry and the Lion Salt Works (admission charge) shows you how lump salt is made, by evaporation of brine. On the same site, the Groundwork Discovery Centre (free admission) gives information on exploring the area.

Marbury country park (free admission)
The country park makes use of the grounds of the now demolished Marbury Hall and gives access to the southern edge of Budworth Mere, where there's a public bird hide for viewing the waterfowl and other birds which inhabit the reedbeds. The reedbeds and the woods to the west are a Cheshire Wildlife Trust reserve.

The Trent and Mersey Canal borders the country park and provides a pleasant link between the Anderton boat lift and the Lion Salt Works/Discovery Centre.

Budworth Mere
Cheshire is renowned for its huge number of meres, ponds and pools. The larger meres were formed in hollows left by retreating glaciers or, in this area in particular, in depressions created by subsidence due to salt being pumped out as brine from underground reserves. The hollow beneath Budworth Mere may be due to either process, and now shows clearly the different stages of natural in-filling. Water lilies float on the open water, reedbeds straddle the margin, and marsh gradually becomes woodland where peat has built up sufficiently to support the trees.

Little Leigh
It's common for churches on hills to be dedicated to St Michael - this is the first St Michael of many on the cycleway.

31

Food and drink

Pubs along the route.

Some refreshments at Groundwork Discovery Centre. Post office/store in Comberbach (early closing Thursday).

Campsites

1/2 mile off-route: Turn right along A49, look for campsite on left-hand side, between road and river.

Woodbine Cottage Caravan Park (takes tents), Acton Bridge, Northwich, Cheshire CW8 3QB, tel: 01606 852319 or 77900. WCs, hot showers, laundry facilities, washing machine.

Cycle spares/repairs

Hartford Cycles, 22 Greenbank Lane, Hartford (nr Northwich), tel: 01606 76170.

Jack Gee Cycles, 136-140 Witton St, Northwich, Cheshire, tel: 01606 43029.

Nearest railway station

Cuddington, Greenbank, Northwich and Lostock Gralam (Chester - Manchester line).

Hartford (Crewe - Liverpool line).

Looking east over Wildboarclough from the top of Shutlingsloe, summer view *(Stage 9)*

Cross 'O the Moor *(Stage 10)*

Astbury church and village green, April *(Stage 12)*

Apart from a short section of B road, this stage keeps to the quiet lanes until Knutsford has to be negotiated, where busier roads leading into and out of the town are inevitable.

The first village is Great Budworth, picturesque enough to linger in, which is just as well, as you'll probably want to recover your breath after the short steep approach. The main road is lined with Cheshire's trade mark, black and white houses, with the added interest of different chimney designs. Village stocks still stand outside the church.

The broad lane looping around to Knutsford takes you past several small ponds, another Cheshire speciality, and a rose nursery at Bates Heath, which provides a colourful sight in summer. It's only after joining the B road that you are returned with a jolt to the modern pace of life, with the roar from the nearby traffic on the M6 and the sight of airliners from Manchester Airport hanging low in the air. But this prepares you for bustling Knutsford, where there's plenty to interest the visitor.

Tourist information
Tourism Officer, Amenities and Recreation Dept, Vale Royal Borough Council, Wyvern House, The Drumber, Winsford, Cheshire, tel: 01606 862862.
Knutsford TIC, Council Offices, Toft Rd, Knutsford, Cheshire WA16 6TA, tel: 01565 632611/632210.
Knutsford Heritage Centre, 90a King St, Knutsford, Cheshire, tel: 01565 650506
Tatton Park, Knutsford, Cheshire WA16 6QN, tel: 01565 750250 (Infoline), 01565 654822 (General Enquiries).
Arley Hall and Gardens, Nr Northwich, Cheshire CW9 6NA, tel: 01565 777353/777284.

Great Budworth village
The black and white houses here date from the 17th century and many were renovated by the local landowning family (the Egerton-Warburtons of Arley Hall) in the 19th century. One member of this family, Rowland (1804-91), was nicknamed the rhyming squire of Arley, because of his predilection for writing verse, some of which can be found in Great Budworth. Have

a look in the Dene Wellhouse and the hotel porch for samples.

Dene Wellhouse (at A559 crossroads), **Great Budworth**
This was built in 1880 (paid for by the Egerton-Warburtons) and shelters the local source of drinking water, which was the only one until 1934, when a piped supply was laid on. Imagine toiling back up the hill with every drop of water that you needed.

St Mary and All Saints church, Great Budworth
The square tower (dating from the 1500s) of this church is a landmark for miles around. The church was once of great importance with a huge parish extending south beyond Nantwich and north to the River Mersey. Additions over the years mean that it displays a variety of architectural styles. It contains 13th century oak stalls (the oldest in Cheshire) and has a small photographic display of renovation work on the roof timbers.

Arley Hall and Gardens, Great Budworth (admission charge)
Home of the Egerton-Warburton family for over 500 years, with gardens open to the public and refreshments

available. There's also a craft centre here.

The rhyming squire, Rowland Egerton-Warburton, wrote songs and verses for the amusement of fellow members of Tarporley Hunt Club. These were collected and published in 1846 as Hunting Songs. His rhyming signposts are to be seen in the grounds of the hall.

Pinfold (on corner of Cann Lane), **Aston-by-Budworth**
Just past the phone box, on the corner of Cann Lane, there's a low-walled enclosure with a plaque attached, noting its architectural features. A pinfold is a place for impounding stray animals and this one is thought to date from the 18th century.

Tatton Park, Knutsford
The park is owned by National Trust and run by Cheshire County Council (admission charge). There's enough here to keep you occupied for several days, never mind several hours. It's a country estate with a thousand acres of deer-park, meres, an authentic Japanese garden, a medieval hall (the Old Hall), a Georgian mansion (Tatton Hall) and a 1930s farm, not forgetting the tea rooms. The park is open daily but the buildings and gardens are closed on Mondays, except Bank Holiday Mondays.

Directions

Cross busy A559 (Northwich to Warrington road).

Cycle through Great Budworth.

Left at T junction.

Detour right for campsite (1 mile)

Continue along lane to Bate Heath.

Detour second left for Arley Hall (signposted) (1 mile)

Left at T junction (onto B5391).

Straight ahead at crossroads with A556 (Dismount).

Right into Manchester Rd.

Detour straight on for Tatton Hall and Park (300yds to park, 2 miles to hall)

Straight on at roundabout.

Straight on at first set of traffic lights.

Left at next set of traffic lights (signposted A537 to Macclesfield).

CARE - Be ready for uphill section to traffic lights just around the corner.

Straight on at traffic lights (right-hand lane) for A537 to Macclesfield.

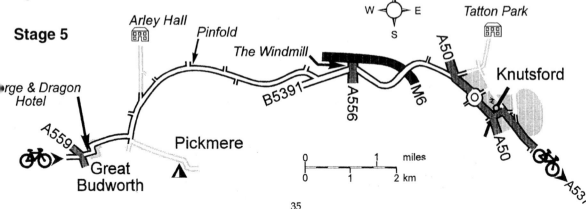

35

Knutsford

Knutsford Heritage Centre (free admission) has plenty of information on the town and surrounding area, with exhibitions and talks given throughout the year.

Knutsford is thought to have gained its name from King Canute, who is also thought to have given rise to the tradition of scattering coloured sands on the ground at weddings. The tale is that King Canute crossed a nearby ford and scattered sand from his shoes, just as a wedding party passed by. Coloured sand is also scattered on the ground on May Day, when the beginning of summer is celebrated here in impressive style.

The town had a silk industry in the 18th century and became an important coaching town before the railways were built. Its claim to fame is that it is the birth and burial place of authoress Elizabeth Gaskell (1810-1865) whose book *Cranford* was based on the town and its inhabitants.

When you're exploring the town, take a look at the railway station at the end of King St. The pavement here is very narrow on one side. This was once the only pavement and was financed by Lady Jane Stanley around the end of the 18th century with money bequeathed for its upkeep on the condition that it was never more than one paving stone wide. She disliked couples walking arm-in-arm.

Food and drink

Pubs along the route.

Village shop on crossroads of B591 and minor road between Pickmere and Higher Wincham.

Knutsford (early closing Wednesday) including Booths supermarket with a cafe at its entrance, enabling you to keep an eye on the cycle while you refresh yourself. Arley Hall and Tatton Hall also offer refreshments.

Campsites

1 mile off-route: After turning right off cycleway, turn first left for Pickmere; enquire at Mereview Farm close to site.

Pickmere Lake Caravan Park (takes tents), Pickmere, nr Knutsford, Cheshire, tel: 01565 733221. WCs, hot showers, laundry facilities.

Cycle spares/repairs

Bikes 'n' Gear, 31 King St, Knutsford, Cheshire WA16 6DW, tel: 01565 750273.

Nearest railway station

Lostock Gralam (Chester - Manchester line).
Knutsford (Chester - Manchester line).

After the pull out of Knutsford along the main road, the gradient slackens and it doesn't take long to reach Ollerton, where you turn off onto quiet lanes again. If the traffic makes you nervous, you may be tempted to take the illegal route along the quiet pavement which runs from the mini-roundabout. If you do, be considerate to any pedestrians.

The lanes wind between the fields, eventually giving you the first of many views of the gritstone hill of Shutlingsloe. You'll be cycling past this on Stage 9. The hill stands at 1660ft (506m) above sea level, just within the Peak National Park on the eastern edge of the county. You'll soon realise that it's a landmark from all directions, although its shape appears to change when viewed from different points along the cycleway. From some aspects it appears as a flat-topped cone; from others a mini-Matterhorn.

Tourist information

Knutsford TIC, Council Offices, Toft Rd, Knutsford, Cheshire WA16 6TA, tel: 01565 632611/632210.

Wilmslow Information Centre, Council Offices, South Drive, Wilmslow, Cheshire, tel: 01625 522275.

Macclesfield TIC, Macclesfield Borough Council, Town Hall, Macclesfield, Cheshire SK10 1DX, tel: 01625 504114/5.

Nether Alderley Mill - for opening times, tel: 01625 523012.

Great Warford Baptist Chapel, Merrymans Lane, Great Warford

As soon as the ban on dissenting religious groups was lifted, those who had worshipped in secret in a local farmhouse converted this ancient cottage and barn into a chapel, in 1712. The oak frames of the early Tudor (mid-16th century) barn remain visible at the rear, although the original wattle and daub infill has been replaced with bricks. A public footpath which runs along the left-hand side of the building gives a good view - do keep to the footpath though.

The chapel originally occupied the whole building,

*Great Warford
Baptist Chapel*

but now only the right-hand side (as you look from the road) is used for worship. The furniture in here is original and worth a peek through the window. Even better, the key-holder may be at home (details on the noticeboard in Warford Crescent, further along the lane, on the left) and able to show you the interior.

Soss Moss Lane

Moss is the local name for a wet and/or peaty area, and although most have been drained, some survive as nature reserves. Some mosses form where hollows fill with sphagnum moss, creating a floating mat over

38

Directions

Cycle uphill on A537

Straight on at mini-roundabout

Left at Ollerton (into Marthall Lane, signposted Mobberley).

First right turn (into Pinfold Lane).

First left (into Kell Green Lane).

Left at T junction.

Right at T junction (into Merrymans Lane), after the Stag's Head.

Right onto A535 (Alderley Edge to Holmes Chapel Road).

First left (into Soss Moss Lane).

Keep left at fork after crossing railway bridge.

Detour right at fork, then right onto A34, for Nether Alderley mill and church (1/2 mile)

Cross A34 (into Artists Lane).

Detour left for Alderley Edge village (1 mile)

Stage 6

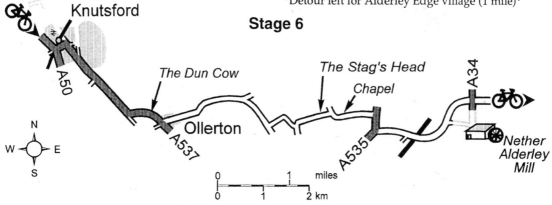

39

deep water. Others are raised peat mosses on originally level sites, and these have been exploited by peat workings, past and present. Lindow Moss near Wilmslow is a famous example, where ancient Lindow Man was found buried in the peat.

Nether Alderley

Nether Alderley is a very old settlement, close to an important Saxon east-west trade route which crossed the main north-south route (now the A34) at Artists Lane. Nether means lower and Alderley means Aldred's leah, i.e. meadow.

Nether Alderley Mill (National Trust, admission charge)

On the east side of the A34 is the oldest of Cheshire's restored water-powered corn mills (the others are at Stretton - also on the cycle route, and Bunbury). The present building has Tudor roof timbers and contains machinery from the 1850s which was originally used to grind corn from the Alderley estate, owned by the Stanley family. There are two huge waterwheels, one above the other, driven by water flowing from the dammed pool behind and above the mill, at roof level. Occasionally flour milling is demonstrated.

St Mary's church, Nether Alderley

The church is at the end of the lane, nearly opposite the mill. It dates from the 14th and 15th centuries and the surprise inside is the Jacobean pew (the Stanley pew) perched on a wall. The pew is in fact a two-storied addition to the church, with a room behind and access from outside, via steps to the right of the porch. Next to the church stands the old school, dating from the 17th century with additions in 1817.

Food and drink

Pubs along the route.
Knutsford and Alderley Edge (early closing Wednesday).
Village shop opposite the Stag's Head sells sandwiches.

Campsites

None on route. See Stages 5 and 7.

Cycle spares/repairs

Bikes 'n' Gear, 31 King St, Knutsford, Cheshire WA16 6DW, tel: 01565 750273.

Nearest railway station

Knutsford (Chester - Manchester line).
Alderley Edge (Crewe - Manchester line).

The transition from plain to gritstone hills is apparent on this stage, with a few steep sections to warm you up for the long climb out of Bollington in Stage 8.

The first hill is in Artists Lane, with two steep sections taking you up to the wooded escarpment of Alderley Edge. If you glance to your left across a field you'll see a barren area, unable to support any vegetation due to the poisonous levels of minerals in old spoil heaps. Once across the B road, the woods are worth exploring for their beauty, unexpected views and the legacy of old mine-workings.

It's a wonderful downhill run along the back road to Prestbury and if you are able to look around, you'll spot the modern mansions built for the wealthy in this exclusive corner of Cheshire. Prestbury is a pretty village with interesting buildings, so don't whizz through and miss them.

Tourist information
Wilmslow Information Centre, Council Offices, South Drive, Wilmslow, Cheshire, tel: 01625 522275.

Macclesfield TIC, Macclesfield Borough Council, Town Hall, Macclesfield, Cheshire SK10 1DX, tel: 01625 504114/5.
The Wizard Country Restaurant/Tea rooms, Macclesfield Rd, Nether Alderley, Macclesfield, Cheshire SK10 4UB, tel: 01625 584000.
Hare Hill Gardens, Prestbury, Cheshire, tel: 01625 828981

Alderley Edge escarpment (National Trust, free admission)
This area has been exploited since the Bronze Age for copper, and miles of shafts and levels were dug in the 18th and 19th centuries to extract copper and cobalt ores. The small, isolated building that you may have noticed opposite The Wizard is where the miners stored their explosives, well away from other buildings, just in case.

The abandoned mines proved to be a death trap for adventurous youngsters. As a result, all of the entrances were sealed up, and the mines leased to Derbyshire

Caving Club, whose members have cut two new shafts into the labyrinth, fixed ladders inside and act as guides to many groups wishing to see the workings. A permanent exhibition (free admission) of the sights below ground is sited near the car park and is usually open at weekends.

The Wizard legend

A farmer from Mobberley crossed Alderley Edge on his way to market to sell his white horse. An old man appeared and offered to buy the animal, but the farmer refused. However, he couldn't sell the animal, and on his return journey he again met the old man, who took him past certain landmarks until they reached the Iron Gates. This hidden entrance in the rock led to a cavern of sleeping warriors, all but one with a white horse, waiting to be called upon to ride and save England. The farmer agreed to sell his horse, and the Wizard paid him three times its value, from the underground store of treasure.

There's a theory that this legend refers to the rich source of copper ores beneath the Edge and that the list of landmarks in the legends refer to the sites of Bronze Age mine pits. But the tale has only been traced back to the mid-17th century. It was probably first printed in around 1805, coinciding with the period when various mining companies exploited the deposits. It's likely that the story was further spread once the railway arrived at the nearby village and the population grew. The Wizard legend formed the basis of a modern children's story by the author Alan Garner, who has claimed (in the March 1991 issue of *Cheshire Life*) that it was his great-great-grandfather Robert Garner, a local stonemason, who carved an inscription and the face of a wizard on the rock known as the Wizard's Well. He was also supposed to be responsible for erecting the so-called Druid's circle in the woods, because he had some stones to dispose of. He must have been energetic and obtained great enjoyment from practical jokes, because these are not small stones to be moved lightly around the countryside.

Alderley Edge village

This prosperous area contains many fine Victorian houses built for Manchester cotton magnates as a result of an incentive from London and North Western Railway in the 1840s to encourage use of the new line. The company offered a free rail pass, valid for 21 years, between Alderley and Manchester, for anyone who built a residence with a rateable value of at least £50

Stage 7

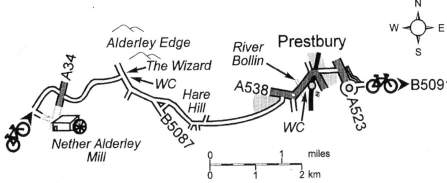

Directions

Cycle up Artists Lane.

Right at T junction (onto B5087).

Detour left for Alderley Edge village (1¹/₂ miles)

First left (signposted Hare Hill).

Detour straight on for Macclesfield (4¹/₂ miles)

Left at T junction (signposted Hare Hill).

Right at T junction (onto A538).

Left at mini-roundabout.

At right-hand bend of main road, take minor road straight on.

Detour on A538 for Macclesfield (3 miles), campsite (4¹/₂ miles)

43

within one mile of Alderley station.

Hare Hill gardens (National Trust, admission charge)
Although pleasant enough for most of the year, these woodland gardens surrounding a walled garden are at their most spectacular in May, when rhododendrons flower in a blaze of vibrant colour.

Prestbury

The name is derived from Priest's Town, which is appropriate because the parish of St Peter's was one of the largest in the country.

The Priest's House, Prestbury

Now a bank, this striking black and white house on the left-hand side of the main street, opposite the church, was once the vicarage, dating back to the 16th century. It fell into disrepair but fortunately was restored in the late 1960s.

St Peter's church, Prestbury

Even if you have no interest in churches (this one was begun in 1220), do wander around the beautifully wooded churchyard. This is a very old site of worship, as evidenced by an 8th century preaching cross, found in fragments in the church walls during renovation in 1841. The cross commemorates the first teaching of Christianity and it's thought that the pieces had been incorporated in the church wall for 400 years. The cross is now on display in a glass case in the churchyard, behind the church. Nearby is the Norman chapel, dating from 1190 and restored in the 18th century. As a consequence much is not original, but the doorway topped with its row of weathered figures is. Have a peep inside and step back 700 years in time.

Food and drink

Pubs along the route.
The Wizard restaurant (not open daily).
The Wizard tearooms, further along farm drive (open Sunday afternoons).
Usually a catering van on Alderley Edge car park at weekends in high season.
Alderley Edge village, Prestbury and Bollington (all early closing Wednesday).

Campsites

$4^{1}/_{2}$ miles off-route: Continue into Macclesfield on A538 (keep off the A523 by-pass) and take the A523 to Leek, turning left at traffic lights (signposted Sutton Lane

Ends). Look for campsite on left once you've cycled beneath the canal at Gurnett. Alternatively, take a train from Prestbury to Macclesfield. Turn left out of the station and take road signs for Leek and Sutton Lane Ends.

Jarman Farm, Sutton, Macclesfield, Cheshire, SK11 0HJ, tel: 01260 252501. WCs, hot showers.

Cycle spares/repairs

Tom Royle Cycles, 105 Brook Lane, Alderley Edge, tel: 01625 585141.

Bikes, 80 Park Lane, Macclesfield, Cheshire, tel: 01625 611375.

Deeside Cycles, 10 Chester Rd, Macclesfield, Cheshire, tel: 01625 433247.

Cycle hire

Groundwork Trust Discovery Centre, Adelphi Mill Gate Lodge, Grimshaw Lane, Bollington, Macclesfield, Cheshire SK10 5JB, tel: 01625 572681.

Nearest railway station

Alderley Edge (Crewe - Manchester line).
Prestbury (Stoke-on-Trent - Stockport line).

Prestbury to Kerridge-end (4¼ miles)

This stage is strenuous, with a lot of uphill work, interspersed with exhilarating downhill runs. Not only have you left the plain behind, but also the black and white houses and the dairy farms. The cycleway takes you to an area of grazing sheep and solid stone buildings, built to withstand the harsher weather.

The first hurdle is the A523. Traffic pours off the by-pass around Macclesfield onto this road, making it difficult to cross. The route then takes you through the old mill town of Bollington and sends you abruptly up an unexpectedly steep haul, leading over the Macclesfield Canal and then on, ever upwards, through the terraced streets and along the much quarried Kerridge Hill. The area is fascinating for those interested in the early industrial revolution, with mills sited wherever water power could be harnessed.

The reward for the climb is the views over the plain to Manchester in the north, Manchester Airport in the east, Macclesfield in the south-west and, further out, the overgrown satellite dish of Jodrell Bank. The cycleway passes within a few miles of Jodrell Bank in Stage 11. The route descends from the ridge by way of an unpleasantly steep and narrow lane with a hairpin bend onto the main road.

If you can't face the hills in this and the next stage, opt out at Macclesfield Canal. A gate at the side of the canal to the left of the bridge gives access to the towpath. Turn right and cycle along here for about 4 miles, leaving the towpath after the aqueduct at the road bridge just west of Gurnett, near a garden centre. Continue along the lane in the same direction and go straight on at the crossroads to pick up the cycleway on the Old Leek Rd (Stage 10).

Tourist information

Macclesfield TIC, Macclesfield Borough Council, Town Hall, Macclesfield, Cheshire SK10 1DX, tel: 01625 504114/5.

Discovery Centre, Grimshaw Lane, Bollington, Nr Macclesfield, Cheshire SK10 5JB, tel: 01625 572681.

Macclesfield and Vale Royal Groundwork Trust - as above.

Directions

Right at T junction onto London Rd (A523).

If the junction is impossibly busy, dismount and walk right, along the main road, to cross further along.

Left at roundabout onto B5091.

Left at Cock & Pheasant pub (onto Bollington Rd).

Continue through Bollington.

Right after the Dog & Partridge pub into Hurst Rd.

Detour right along canal for campsite (4½ miles) and to avoid hilly stages

Left at T junction (at end of Hurst Lane).

Right at T junction (onto Jacksons Lane).

Left at Bull's Head pub (into Redway).

* Detour on foot to White Nancy (100yds)*

Left turn (into Lidgetts Lane).

CARE - Descend very steep hill to a busy main road.

Turn left (onto A5002).

Take second of the two right turns at row of cottages in dip (into Penny Lane).

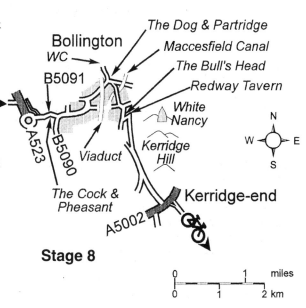

Bollington
WC
B5091
The Dog & Partridge
Maccesfield Canal
The Bull's Head
Redway Tavern
White Nancy
Kerridge Hill
Viaduct
A523
B5090
The Cock & Pheasant
Kerridge-end
A5002

Stage 8

0   1   miles
0   1   2 km

Lukic Belgrade Country House Hotel, Jackson Lane, Kerridge, Bollington, Macclesfield, Cheshire, tel: 01625 573246.

Bollington

In its heyday this mill town had 13 mills run by family businesses. Macclesfield Canal gave a further boost to the town and many 19th century shops and cottages survive, giving a good impression of the town as it was.

Middlewood Way (free admission)

The Middlewood Way began life in 1869 as the Macclesfield, Bollington and Marple railway. But it declined with competition from the roads and closed in 1970. Now it's managed by the local council's rangers for recreation and wildlife value. Cycling is permitted and the way offers a traffic-free route towards Macclesfield to the south and Marple to the north. Watch out for pedestrians and horseriders though.

Macclesfield Canal

This was one of the last canals to be built in Britain, opening in 1831 when railways were coming into their own. However, it remained successful for many years, carrying coal, silk, cotton and stone along the eastern edge of Cheshire, linking the Potteries with Marple, on the edge of Manchester.

Kerridge Hill, Bollington

This long ridge has been quarried for its sandstone for at least 500 years and there is still one quarry in operation. There were also coal mines here which exploited the seams that outcropped on the hillside. Drift mines were dug into the hillside to extract the coal but only on a small scale. The last closed down in 1926.

Chimney, Windmill Lane, Kerridge Hill, Bollington

On the right you can see the top of a chimney that was marked on early maps as Victoria Engine Chimney, presumably taking its name from Victoria Bridge nearby. Apparently the bridge once bore the date 24th May 1837, the date of Queen Victoria's birthday and the year of her accession. It's possible that this was the year that the tramway below the bridge was opened. If you look over the bridge parapet you'll see the tramway that necessitated the bridge. Kerridge Tramway was built by the owner of Endon Quarries to move stone down to the newly constructed Macclesfield Canal. This extremely steep section may have used gravity engines or steam winding engines, which would explain the existence of the chimney. A public footpath descends beneath the bridge and alongside the incline, if you fancy exploring further. The gradient eases off on the other side of the cottage, but you've got to climb back up all of those steps again. There are supposed to be 118, but we lost count.

Windmill site, Kerridge Hill

Windmill Lane did have a windmill once, which was used to grind corn, but it was demolished in the 1940s. It originally stood on Macclesfield Common and was moved to Kerridge Hill in the early 1800s. It was sited in front of the row of cottages set back from the road on the left, close to a quarry entrance. If you walk along the public footpath, which leaves the quarry track on the right and heads for the side of the cottages, you can see the site better.

White Nancy, Kerridge Hill, Bollington

To see White Nancy, and the tremendous view from Kerridge Hill, walk (no cycling permitted) along the public footpath that leads out of the Redway Tavern car park and follow it uphill.

White Nancy was a functional folly, designed to be used as a summerhouse and containing a circular stone table and stone benches. Once open-sided, it has now been blocked up to curb vandalism. This 20ft high white-painted dome stands 918ft (280m) above sea level at the northern end of Kerridge Hill and was built in 1817 to commemorate the Battle of Waterloo. Quite why it should be called White Nancy is a mystery and various theories have been put forward. Two of the most feasible are that it was either named after a lady of the Gaskell family (who paid for the monument) or named after the leading horse of the team of eight that dragged the table up the hill.

Food and drink

Pubs along the route.

Shop and bakery/delicatessen on main road through Bollington (early closing Wednesday).

Lukic-Belgrade Country House Hotel and Restaurant, on Jacksons Lane, serves light meals.

Campsites

4½ miles off-route: Turn right along canal towpath to Gurnett, leave canal at first road bridge after the aqueduct. Double back along the lane, turn right, look for campsite on left.

THE CHESHIRE CYCLEWAY

Jarman Farm, Sutton, Macclesfield, Cheshire, SK11
0HJ, tel: 01260 252501. WCs, hot showers.
Also at Wildboarclough, see Stage 9.

Cycle spares/repairs
Bikes, 80 Park Lane, Macclesfield, Cheshire, tel: 01625
611375.
Deeside Cycles, 10 Chester Rd, Macclesfield, Cheshire,
tel: 01625 433247.

Cycle hire
Groundwork Trust, Discovery Centre, Grimshaw Lane,
Bollington, Nr Macclesfield, Cheshire SK10 5JB, tel:
01625 572681.

Nearest railway station
Prestbury (Stoke-on-Trent - Stockport line).
Macclesfield (Stoke-on-Trent - Stockport line).

More uphill work along Penny Lane leads to the main road to Buxton, which unfortunately cannot be avoided, although the time on it can be reduced by taking a short cut, if you don't mind missing some of the views.

You're well into the gritstone hills now, and there's no mistaking it, with a steady climb for nearly 2 miles. But the reward on a fine day is a tremendous vista of wild moorland and isolated valleys, with a view of Shining Tor, which at 1834ft (559m) above sea level is the highest point in Cheshire.

Other landmarks include the appropriately named crag of Windgather at the northern end of the ridge and closer, the gap called Oldgate Nick, which implies an old route through the hills, probably used by mule trains carrying salt. The lonely building on the skyline ahead is the Cat & Fiddle, England's second highest inn at 1657ft (505m).

To the right, the telecommunications tower on top of Sutton Common dominates. Further right, the tips of the conifers of Macclesfield Forest are visible on the skyline.

After cycling slightly further on, Lamaload reservoir and its ugly dam come into view on the left. Then it's another downhill swoop along the beautiful, lonely Wildboarclough valley.

Tourist information
Macclesfield TIC, Macclesfield Borough Council, Town Hall, Macclesfield, Cheshire SK10 1DX, tel: 01625 504114/5.
Discovery Centre, Grimshaw Lane, Bollington, Nr Macclesfield, Cheshire SK10 5JB, tel: 01625 572681.
Brookside Cafe, Wildboarclough, Cheshire, tel: 01260 227632.

Tegg's Nose country park (free admission)
This is sited at one of the largest quarries in the area, eventually closed in 1955. There's a small shelter, information point, WC and refreshment kiosk (open during busy periods) and an hour's worth of quarrying displays. A circuit of the country park will take you 2 hours to walk (cycling not permitted).

Shutlingsloe from east

A537

This is a relatively new road, authorised in 1821 to follow a better line than the older 1758 turnpike road. The section of A road after the Setter Dog pub coincides with the old route, which the cycleway follows when it leaves the A road to climb uphill before dropping down into Wildboarclough.

Macclesfield Forest chapel

This is one of a few churches which continues the tradition of rush-bearing. The practice dates back to the times when churches had earth floors that were strewn with rushes. These were renewed annually with a ceremony, which is held here every August.

Macclesfield Forest (free admission)
This area of coniferous plantation is owned by North West Water and surrounds the two reservoirs of

Directions

Left at T junction onto main road (A537 Macclesfield to Buxton).

Detour right, opposite Setter Dog, to Tegg's Nose country park (1/2 mile)

Detour second right after Setter Dog to Charity Lane, signposted a dead-end, but offering a bumpy short cut to Forest chapel, where you go straight on at the crossroads of lanes and track, turn left, then right to regain cycleway

Third right after Setter Dog.

Right at T junction.

Right at next T junction.

Detour straight on for Stanley Arms pub (few yards)

Detour first right, then first right again up 1 in 5 hill to Forest chapel (3/4 mile)

Keep straight on through the valley to Wildboarclough village.

Detour for campsite (2 miles)

Pass row of cottages (Edinboro Row) on right.

Detour left over Clough Brook bridge for village (300yds)

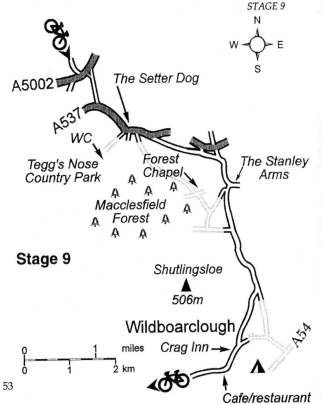

53

Trentabank and Ridgegate. The original Macclesfield Forest encompassed a much larger area, of around 95 square miles. The earliest reference to it was in the mid-12th century and the first dated description of the forest boundary was in 1619. It was defined by the rivers Mersey, Goyt and Dane, but the western boundary followed no natural feature. It's thought possible that some old boundary marks may be associated with the forest, including Cross O' the Moor near Sutton, which the cycleway passes. As with Delamere Forest, the area was a deer forest but unlike Delamere there was only limited tree growth, due to the height above sea level. In 1684 the Earl of Derby acquired the pastures and the forest became an administrative area only. There's an information point and WCs by

Looking south to Sutton Common and telecommunications tower from Tegg's Nose, summer view

Trentabank reservoir, but only detour here if you can face the steep and narrow lane back onto the cycleway.

Wildboarclough
Clough is the local name for a valley. This area suffered a flash flood in May 1989, when a ferocious thunderstorm, accompanied by torrential rain, caused the brook to rise high enough to sweep away drystone walls and scour vegetation from valley's floor. All has now been restored and a plaque on the bridge over Clough Brook commemorates the event.

Wildboarclough hamlet
There's little here to show for an industry which was here for just over a century. In the early 1800s, a cotton factory was constructed on the brook, with an upper and lower works. Dyehouses were built, plus two rows of workers' cottages; Edinboro Cottages in the valley, and Glasgow Cottages higher up, along the lane beside the church. If you walk over the bridge across Clough Brook, you'll see the large building called the Old Post Office. This was the administrative part of the mill complex that escaped demolition in the 1950s. Now the only industry in the area is the spring-water bottling plant next to the Crag Inn.

Food and drink
Pubs along the route.
Tegg's Nose (refreshment kiosk in busy periods).
Brookside Cafe, Wildboarclough.

Campsites
2 miles off-route: Take left fork by a car park (with Clough House farm buildings beyond it). Turn left to A54, turn right onto A54 and look for farm at the end of a long drive to the right.
Berry Bank Farm, Wildboarclough, Macclesfield SK11 0BG, tel: 01260 227280. WC, washbasin (cold water only).

Cycle spares/repairs
None on route.
See Stage 8.

Nearest railway station
Macclesfield (Stoke-on-Trent - Stockport line).

Wildboarclough to Lower Pexhill (7³/₄ miles)

After the exhilarating ride down through Wildboarclough, the uphill route out of the valley comes as a shock. We found it impossible to cycle the 300yds of narrow, winding 1 in 5 lane and had to get off and push. According to the map, the gradient slackens off to about 1 in 20 for the next 600yds, but it didn't feel very much easier after our exertions on the first section. The only consolation is the views looking back over flat-topped Shutlingsloe on the left and a gritstone edge (the Roaches) away on the right.

The crest of the hill is marked by an old stone cross - it probably marks the spot where medieval travellers and their pack animals gasped their last.

Here the world is spread out before you with Macclesfield Forest in view across the fields behind the cross; the rubble-strewn face of Tegg's Nose quarry overlooking it. In the other direction there's the telecommunications tower on Sutton Common, and to its left, Bosley Cloud, with Mow Cop beyond. Between is the Cheshire plain, with Jodrell Bank, wooded Alderley Edge, aircraft at Manchester Airport, and the Lancashire hills all clearly visible.

The resulting run downhill to the Church House Inn is as enjoyable as the uphill struggle was miserable. But don't go so fast that you overshoot the hairpin bend after the Hanging Gate Inn. Don't go so fast that you miss the glorious views either. Stop now and then to savour the moorland landscape, before you return to the plain and its milder scenery.

Time this stage to avoid arriving in Sutton Lane Ends at the same time that the local engineering works close (around 4-4.30pm). The workforce race home through the narrow lanes as if only they were on the roads, which is disconcerting to say the least.

Tourist information

Macclesfield TIC, Macclesfield Borough Council, Town Hall, Macclesfield, Cheshire SK10 1DX, tel: 01625 504114/5.

Discovery Centre, Grimshaw Lane, Bollington, Nr

Directions

Right at fork on sharp left-hand bend.

Right at T junction.

Left at Church House Inn.

Detour for campsite (300yds), Gurnett village (¹/₂ mile) and Macclesfield (2 miles)

Straight on at staggered crossroads (into Walker Lane).

Cycle through village.

First left (into Parvey Lane).

Left at T junction (into Old Leek Rd).

Straight on at crossroads with A523.

Right at T junction in Warren.

Detour left for Maggoty's Wood (300yds) and Gawsworth Hall (¹/₂ mile)

Straight on at crossroads with A536 (into Dark Lane).

CARE - listen before crossing, traffic approaches this junction at speed.

Left at T junction onto B5392.

Stage 10

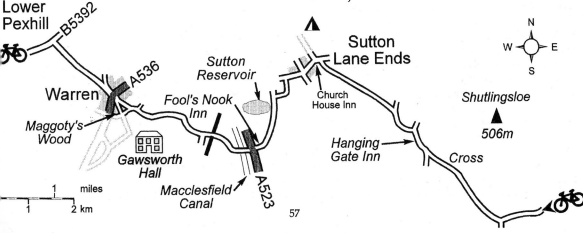

Macclesfield, Cheshire SK10 5JB, tel: 01625 572681.
Gawsworth Hall, Macclesfield, Cheshire, tel: 01260 223456.

Cross O' the Moor

This wayside cross is also known as Greenway Cross, which indicates its probable function as a waymarker. It's also been suggested that it marks the edge of the old hunting forest of Macclesfield. It's thought to be medieval and is hewn from red sandstone, which is found to the south of here. It consists of a rough block, with a cross cut in relief on the surface of both sides.

Warren village

Sometimes referred to as Gawsworth Warren, this village takes its name from the rabbit warren of Gawsworth estate. Until relatively recently, rabbits were valued as livestock and farmed for their fur and meat. They were kept in a particular place, with a warrener in charge of their welfare.

Maggoty's Wood (National Trust, free admission)

Old Maggoty was the nickname (behind his back) of Samuel Johnson (1691-1773), dancing-master to local gentry families. His other nickname (to his face) was Lord Flame, due to the part he had played in a London play that he'd written, which made him well known. His wit was in demand and he was one of the last professional jesters in England. He asked to be buried in this wood where he loved to walk. In 1851, the Reverend Edward Massie composed further verses for a slab alongside the grave using words which were more appropriate for Victorian times. The Gawsworth estate was sold in 1920 and the new owner of the wood restored the grave and lettering before giving the site to the National Trust.

Church Lane, Gawsworth

The ghost of Mary Fitton is reputed to walk in this avenue and in the church. She was the daughter of the Fittons, who were the Lords of the Manor of Gawsworth, and became maid of honour to Queen Elizabeth I at the age of 17. She willed that she be interred in the church, but there's no record of her burial, although other members of the family are interred here and their monuments are here, including Mary's.

St James' church, Gawsworth

This was built on the site of a Norman chapel by the Fitton family in the 15th century. The churchyard wall had to be built around the yew tree, which proves the tree to be at least 500 years old.

Gawsworth Old Hall and Gardens (admission charge)
Gawsworth village is old, beautiful and very unusual. There's the glorious black and white mansion with grounds that include a series of rectangular ponds, a medieval rectory and St James' church. There's also what is often referred to as a medieval tilting or jousting ground. There are no cottages or farm buildings to be seen because the hall once stood in its own parkland of some 243 hectares (600 acres). The garden's brick wall was built, at great expense, in Tudor times and a tremendous amount of earth was moved to create the mounds and terraces that can be seen today. It is thought that this garden was designed to stage entertainments on a huge scale to impress and flatter Queen Elizabeth I, if she deigned to stay at the hall, but she never did favour the Fitton family.

Gurnett village
James Brindley, the famous civil engineer and canal builder, was apprenticed here between 1733-1740 to Abraham Bennett. There's a plaque on one of the buildings which marks the site of the millwright's shop, just before the aqueduct, on the northern side of the lane.

Old Leek Rd
This is the route of the old London to Manchester road, a turnpike road authorised in 1762. Turnpike roads were built by trusts who were entitled to charge a toll for those who used the road, so that local residents didn't bear the brunt of providing services for travellers from afar. Where the cycleway turns sharp right toward Fool's Nook Inn, you can see the original line of the road straight ahead. The present A road follows the line of the 1826 road which replaced this hilly section. On the left is a quarry which provided roadstone, extracted by pauper labour from Sutton.

Sutton reservoir
This is one of many British Waterways Board reservoirs in the district. The water is used to keep the canal system topped up - every time a lock is used on the canal to move down a level, some water is lost from the upper section. One way to replace this is by channelling reservoir water into the canal. In this case the water flows along a narrow feeder canal from the dammed end of the reservoir to the nearest point of Macclesfield

Canal. A feeder canal leads to the reservoir too, channelling water from a stream over a mile away.

There's a stone water trough on the left-hand side of the road, before the start of the hill, with the names of the surveyors inscribed on the side with the date, 1836.

Food and drink
Pubs along the route.

Campsites
300yds off-route: Straight on at Church House Inn, look for campsite on the right.
Jarman Farm, Sutton, Macclesfield, Cheshire, SK11 0HJ, tel: 01260 252501. WCs, hot showers.

Cycle spares/repairs
Bikes, 80 Park Lane, Macclesfield, Cheshire, tel: 01625 611375.
Deeside Cycles, 10 Chester Rd, Macclesfield, Cheshire, tel: 01625 433247.

Nearest railway station
Macclesfield (Stoke-on-Trent - Stockport line).

Lower Pexhill to Radnor Bridge (7³/₄ miles)

This stage shuns villages in complete contrast to the previous stage. Now you're in a lush part of the county, even by Cheshire's standards, with rich farmland, mansions surrounded by parks, and ancient black and white churches. There are pleasant, broad-verged lanes to follow, with few hills to trouble you until the descent to the River Dane at Radnor Bridge, which fortunately is steeper to descend to than to ascend from.

Tourist information

Congleton TIC, Town Hall, High St, Congleton, Cheshire CW12 1BN, tel: 01260 271095.

Capesthorne Hall, Macclesfield, Cheshire SK11 9JY, tel: 01625 861221.

A J's Coffee Shop & Restaurant, Church Farm, Marton, Cheshire, tel: 01260 224785.

Jodrell Bank Science Centre and Arboretum, Macclesfield, Cheshire SK11 9DL, tel: 01477 571339.

Capesthorne Hall (admission charge)

This is the home of the Bromley-Davenport family, whose ancestors have been here since Domesday and were the Chief Foresters for Macclesfield, upholding Forest Law. The original half-timbered hall was replaced in the early 1700s, and after a fire, the central portion was rebuilt in the mid 1800s.

All Saints church, Siddington

This old church is hidden from the road at the end of a curving drive, lined with pine trees and rhododendrons, splendidly scarlet when in flower in May and June.

On closer inspection of this black and white church, you'll see that it has been partly bricked and painted black and white to give the impression of half-timbering. This was done in the 18th century, when the timbers rotted, but much of the building is genuine. The original timber framing is thought likely to be 14th century, and the south porch, roof and screen are original, with the pulpit dating from 1633.

St James & St Paul's church, Marton

This is of similar age to All Saints, founded in 1343, and

is claimed to be the oldest timber-framed church in Europe that's still in use. It suffered the same fate as All Saints, being rebuilt in brick in the 18th century due to decaying timbers. The roof was lowered in 1804 and the aisle windows altered later that century. The tower is supported in the belfry by huge timbers and is unusual because it's roofed in wooden shingles.

Marton village

The main road and lanes behind are lined with black and white cottages and the village boasts the largest and probably oldest oak in the county. It once housed a calf shed, then a Wendy house, having a tremendous girth although not a great height. It's thought likely to be over 600 years old.

Jodrell Bank Science Centre and Arboretum
(admission charge)

The huge dish, which is visible from miles away, although more difficult to see from this stage of the cycleway, is a radio telescope that was sited here because there was too much electrical interference in Manchester. Manchester University already had a botanical research station here and the radar equipment was set up from the end of 1945. The telescope with its 249ft (76m) bowl was finished in 1957, in time to track the newly launched Soviet *Sputnik I*, the world's first artificial satellite. The science centre explains the science of space study and, in the grounds, the Environmental Discovery Centre (opened in 1992 by Dr David Bellamy) gives an insight and introduction to the arboretum, which was started in 1972. Amongst the trees grown here are the national collection of flowering and fruiting crab apples (*Malus* species) and the national collection of mountain ash and whitebeams (*Sorbus* species).

Food and drink

Pub and cafe at Marton.
Refreshments at Jodrell Bank Science Centre.
Congleton (early closing Wednesday).

Campsites

None on route.
See Stage 10.

Cycle spares/repairs

Dean's Toys & Cycles, Lawton St post office, Congleton, tel: 01260 273277.
Cycle Clearance Centre, 3 Silk Street, Congleton, Cheshire, tel: 01260 297837.

Nearest railway station

Congleton (Stoke-on-Trent - Stockport line).

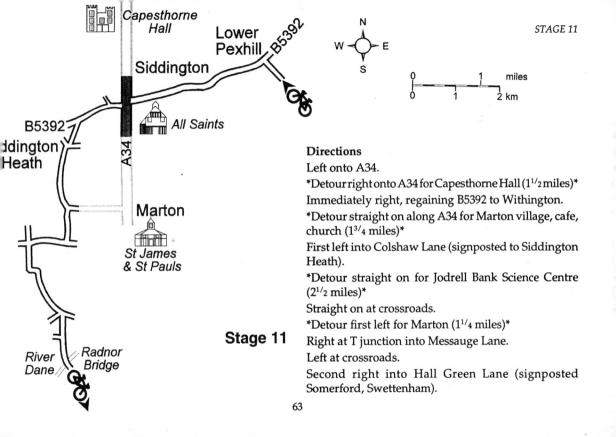

Capesthorne Hall

Lower Pexhill

B5392

Siddington

B5392

All Saints

B5392

Siddington Heath

A34

Marton

St James & St Pauls

Stage 11

River Dane

Radnor Bridge

N
W—E
S

0 ——— 1   miles
0 ——— 1 ——— 2   km

Directions

Left onto A34.

Detour right onto A34 for Capesthorne Hall (1¹/₂ miles)

Immediately right, regaining B5392 to Withington.

Detour straight on along A34 for Marton village, cafe, church (1³/₄ miles)

First left into Colshaw Lane (signposted to Siddington Heath).

Detour straight on for Jodrell Bank Science Centre (2¹/₂ miles)

Straight on at crossroads.

Detour first left for Marton (1¹/₄ miles)

Right at T junction into Messauge Lane.

Left at crossroads.

Second right into Hall Green Lane (signposted Somerford, Swettenham).

Radnor Bridge to Rode Heath (7$^{1}/_{2}$ miles)

The route skirts Congleton before taking a busy A road south. We've included a detour to avoid this route, but keep to the cycleway if you're interested in seeing the unusual church at Astbury, which is especially attractive in spring when the village green is covered in daffodils.

The cycleway leaves the fast traffic on this busy road to follow lanes that offer good views of Mow Cop folly on the ridge to the east. A brief encounter with another busy A road is soon over and you return to another world of peace and quiet, with gorse-covered Lawton Heath on your left, grazed by inquisitive horses on the day that we cycled by.

Tourist information

Congleton TIC, Town Hall, High St, Congleton, Cheshire CW12 1BN, tel: 01260 271095.

Astbury Water Park Ltd, Astbury Lake, Newcastle Rd, Congleton, Cheshire, tel: 01260 299771.

Astbury Tea Shop, Astbury Marsh, Congleton, Cheshire, tel: 01260 277099.

Little Moreton Hall, Congleton, Cheshire CW12 4SD, tel: 01260 272018.

Congleton

Congleton is often referred to as Bear Town, because the money kept for a new town bible was used to buy a bear instead. This was one of last towns to end bear baiting.

Congleton was an established market town in medieval times and despite modern alterations to the town, it still retains its medieval street pattern. The oldest buildings are the medieval Old Kings Arms and two 17th century inns, the White Lion and Lion and Swan, all retaining their half-timbered appearance. The town expanded with the development of the silk industry, and mills were built here in the 18th century. In 1866 an unusual design of town hall was built, in Venetian Gothic style.

St Mary's church, Astbury

The first thing that strikes you about this church is the tower and spire set to the left-hand side of the main body of the building. The church is made of millstone grit and the oldest part dates from the late 13th century.

Lift bridge at Wrenbury *(Stage 15)*

STAGE 12

Directions

Uphill from Radnor Bridge.

Second left (signposted to Congleton).

Detour to avoid A34 - ignore left turn, straight on at crossroads over A54, right onto A534 for third of a mile, first left, straight on at crossroads, re-join route by turning right at Ivy Cottage

Left at T junction (onto A54 Congleton - Holmes Chapel Rd).

First right (into Box Lane).

Detour straight on for pub, take-aways, shops (1/2 mile), Congleton centre (1 1/2 miles)

Straight on at crossroads with A534 (into Padgbury Lane).

Right at T junction onto A34.

*Detour to avoid more of main road, first right, first left at crossroads, pass Brownlow Inn, re-join cycleway

Stretton Watermill

by turning first right at Ivy Cottage*

Second right after car sales on left.

Detour, straight on for Little Moreton Hall (1 mile)

First left (by Ivy Cottage).

Right at T junction.

Right at T junction.

Left onto A50.

Ignore turning to A533 on right.

Next right after A533.

CARE - may be prudent to dismount here and choose your moment to cross.

River Dane

Radnor Bridge

A54

Congleton

A34

A54

A534

Astbury Mere

A527

Heath Farm Inn

Cafe & Restaurant

Cafe

Astbury

Stage 12

Brownlow Inn

Little Moreton Hall

A34

N W E S

Rode Heath A50 A533

miles

km

The detached tower is 14th century but its recessed spire was rebuilt in the mid 1800s. This is another church with a two-storied porch, plus a three-storied porch, which is even more unusual. The carved wooden eagle lectern dates from 1500 and is unique in Cheshire. In the grounds there's an ancient yew, known to be at least 1000 years old.

The church overlooks a village green - a rare sight in Cheshire.

Little Moreton Hall (National Trust, admission charge) This 15th century half-timbered moated hall is considered the most perfect example in the country and is worth visiting even if it's closed, just to see the exterior. The whole building looks as if it's about to collapse, due to the addition of a heavy third storey which caused distortion to the lower timbers almost immediately after it was constructed.

Mow Cop folly (National Trust, free admission) Although not particularly close to the cycleway, the folly is very obvious on this stage. It should be, because it was built in order to improve the view of the ridge from Rode Hall, near Rode Heath. It's one of the earliest examples of a folly in the country, built in 1754 for Randle Wilbraham of Rode Hall. It was probably the latest fashion and would have provided local employment too. Although termed a folly, it did function as a summerhouse and shelter during picnics. Mow Cop is also well known in the chapel world as the birthplace of primitive methodism, on Sunday 31st May 1807.

Food and drink
Congleton (early closing Wednesday).
Astbury Water Park.
Astbury Tea Shop.
Tea rooms at Little Moreton Hall.

Campsites
None on route.
See Stages 9 and 14.

Cycle spares/repair
Cycle Clearance Centre, 3 Silk St, Congleton, Cheshire, tel: 01260 297837.
Dean's Toys & Cycles, Lawton St post office, Congleton, tel: 01260 273277.

Nearest railway station
Congleton (Stoke-on-Trent - Stockport line).

Little Moreton Hall

Rode Heath to Englesea-Brook (6½ miles)

Fairly flat roads take you from the quiet fields around Lawton Heath to the college town of Alsager, small but busy, and then past the roar of traffic on the M6 and what looks like a huge but sinister battery chicken farm on your left. In fact it's British Aerospace's Ordnance Works. The grim modern world and its noise are left behind as you enter olde worlde Barthomley, a picture-postcard maker's dream village. But even this pretty village has a dark past.

Tourist information

Congleton TIC, Town Hall, High St, Congleton, Cheshire CW12 1BN, tel: 01260 271095.
Sandbach TIC, Motorway Service Area, M6 Northbound, Sandbach, Cheshire CW11 0TD, tel: 01270 766611.

Barthomley village

This is an attractive hamlet with half-timbered buildings clustered around the church. The White Lion Inn dates from 1614 and St Bertoline church is mainly 15th century. The church was the scene of an English Civil War massacre by Royalists in the 1640s. They killed 12 villagers who had taken refuge in the tower. The brook which runs alongside the pub is Wulvarn Brook, the name being derived from wolf and echoing the tale that the last wolf in Britain was killed in this area.

Food and drink

Pubs along the route.
Alsager (early closing Wednesday).
Little Chef near M6 junction.

Campsites

None on route.
See stage 14.

Cycle spares/repairs

Sideways Cycles, 131 Talke Rd, Alsager, via Stoke-on-Trent, tel: 01270 883785.

Nearest railway station

Alsager (Stoke-on-Trent - Crewe line).

Directions

Right at crossroads (really a T junction, ahead is a dead-end).

Left at crossroads.

Right at school playing fields (into Lodge Rd, signposted to Leisure Centre and Hassall).

Detour straight on for Alsager's centre (1/2 mile), turn right at traffic lights to re-join cycleway (1/2 mile)

Lodge Rd becomes Chancery Lane.

Left at T junction with Hassall Rd.

Immediately right (onto B5077).

Left at traffic lights.

First right into lane signposted Barthomley.

Detour for cafe, straight on (1/2 mile)

Turn right in Englesea-Brook village.

Stage 13

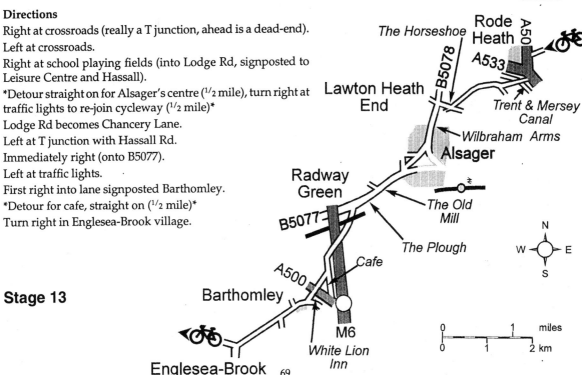

Englesea-Brook to Audlem (9¹/₂ miles)

After the short steep climb along the narrow lane out of Englesea-Brook, it's easy pedalling past many fields of fodder maize alternating with pastures. The route follows the lanes to by-pass the southern edge of Crewe, then takes a well-used B road from Wybunbury that leads onto a fairly quiet A road into Audlem. The lane to Wybunbury gives good views across the fields to the much troubled church tower in the village.

Tourist information

Nantwich TIC, Church House, Church Walk, Nantwich, Cheshire CW5 5RG, tel: 01270 610983/610880.
Dagfields Craft Centre and Farm, Walgherton, nr Nantwich, Cheshire, tel: 01270 841336.

Church tower, Wybunbury

This 96ft (29m) tower without a church has had a troubled history. It was built, with church attached, in the late 15th century but underground springs caused subsidence, so that the church had to be rebuilt five times. At one stage, in the 1830s, the top of the tower was nearly 6ft out of true, which was corrected by digging out clay from beneath the structure so that it moved back. Finally, in 1976, the church was pulled down. By this time, the tower was 4ft out of true again and a specialist firm jacked it up, placed new foundations beneath it, and left it with a deliberate lean (about 2ft out of true), to remain in character. This was completed in 1989.

Wybunbury Moss

The houses lining the road through the village hide a National Nature Reserve from view. This treacherous piece of ground consists of a mat of vegetation growing over deep water. Interesting in its own right (these features are known as Shwing moors or bogs) and a valuable habitat, it's out of bounds without a permit from English Nature, and an escort.

Doddington Hall

You can't fail to miss the lodge gates at the crossroads with the A51, opposite the Boar's Head. These once

Stage 14

Directions

Right at T junction onto A5020.

First left at White Lion Inn (into Cemetery Lane).

Left at crossroads (really a T junction, with dead-end straight ahead) into Weston Lane.

First left into Casey Lane.

Detour straight on to the T junction with the B5071, turn right to Crewe

Straight on at crossroads with Back Lane.

Straight on at crossroads with A52 (into Cobbs Lane).

Right at T junction (signposted to Wybunbury).

Left at T junction (into Bridge St).

Detour right uphill into Wybunbury for the Swan Inn, church tower and picturesque cottages (100yds), continue for Stapeley Water Gardens (2½ miles) and campsite at Nantwich (4¼ miles)

Bear right at top of hill in village.

Cross A51 into Crewe Rd.

Left to Audlem at T junction with A529.

71

watched over one of several drives to Doddington Hall, about 2 miles to the south-east. The hall was built in the late 1700s for the Delves-Broughton family. You may have noticed the family name inscribed on the primary school that you passed at the top of the hill coming out of Wybunbury. The inscription reads 'Delves' Charity School, erected 1822'.

Nantwich

One of the salt towns, this was the only town in Cheshire to support Cromwell and the Parliamentarians against the Royalists in the English Civil War. It has many attractive half-timbered buildings.

Food and drink

Pubs along the route.
Shop in Weston, Wybunbury.
Cafe at Dagfields Craft Centre, Walgherton.
Cafe at Stapeley Water Gardens.
Nantwich (early closing Wednesday).

Church tower, Wybunbury

Cycle spares/repairs

G Carless, 15 Hightown, Crewe, Cheshire, tel: 01270 213642.

Supreme Cycles, 42-48 Earle St, Crewe, Cheshire, tel: 01270 585640.

J E Williams & Son, 17 Edleston Rd, Crewe, tel: 01270 255672.

Campsites

4¼ miles off-route: Cycle through Wybunbury village, take second lane on left on right-hand bend, to Butt Green and Stapeley Water Gardens, turn right onto A51 into Nantwich, head for A534 and take first left after roundabout into

Shrewbridge Rd, cross railway line at level-crossing. Campsite next to park.

Brookfield Caravan Park (takes tents), Shrewbridge Rd, Nantwich, Cheshire, tel: 01270 537777. WCs, hot showers.

Nearest railway station

Crewe (junction of 5 lines).
Nantwich (Crewe - Whitchurch line).

Big Mere and church, Marbury. (Stage 15)

Audlem to Bickley Moss (11½ miles)

Once out of Audlem, the rest of this stage keeps to the lanes, many very quiet, which meander around the countryside through pleasant villages with black and white buildings in abundance. Canals dominate this stage, some crossed by flat lift bridges and others by humpback bridges which are gentler than those encountered in previous stages. The wharf alongside the canal in Audlem is a place to linger, with plenty going on at the staircase of locks. The lift bridge and marina near Wrenbury also provide a pleasant place to take a break.

Tourist information

Nantwich TIC, Church House, Church Walk, Nantwich, Cheshire CW5 5RG, tel: 01270 610983/610880.
Whitchurch TIC, The Civic Centre, High St, Whitchurch, Shropshire SY13 1AX, tel: 01948 664577.

Audlem

Audlem is a lovely old town, which received a charter to run a market in 1295, although this ceased many years ago. The Market Hall in front of the church was built in the 1700s and was sometimes referred to as the Shambles, or Butter Market, although it's not certain what was sold here. It was restored in 1992. The large stone block to the right of the Market Hall is a bear stone, which would once have had an iron ring for tethering the town bear for baiting. The stone is a granite boulder from the last Ice Age, and thought to be either from the Mountains of Mourne in N. Ireland or from the hills of Cumbria. The town also boasts a state-of-the-art superloo, which needs 10p to enter. It's at the entrance to the car park, opposite the fish and chip shop.

St James the Great church, Audlem

This church stands prominently on a hill in the centre of the town, and is thought to be on the site of a Celtic burial ground. The oldest parts of this sandstone building date from the 13th century. On the side of the church there's an ancient mass dial (one of only five in Cheshire) which in Saxon times would have determined the time of church services.

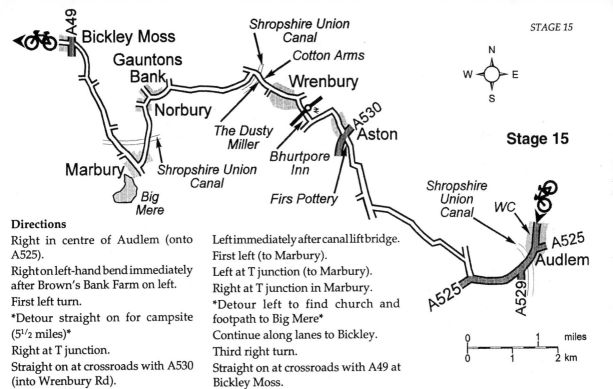

Stage 15

Directions

Right in centre of Audlem (onto A525).

Right on left-hand bend immediately after Brown's Bank Farm on left.

First left turn.

Detour straight on for campsite (5½ miles)

Right at T junction.

Straight on at crossroads with A530 (into Wrenbury Rd).

Left at T junction.

Left immediately after canal lift bridge.

First left (to Marbury).

Left at T junction (to Marbury).

Right at T junction in Marbury.

Detour left to find church and footpath to Big Mere

Continue along lanes to Bickley.

Third right turn.

Straight on at crossroads with A49 at Bickley Moss.

75

Shropshire Union Canal

This canal, known as the Shroppie, was built by Telford in 1828 and here boats climb out of the county via 15 locks. The change in levels is 93ft (28m), achieved over 1¼ miles. This section is the Birmingham to Liverpool branch where the last mule and horse-drawn traffic ceased in 1954, now replaced by powered leisure craft. The canal-side pub, the Shroppie Fly, was converted from a wharfman's house in the 1970s; here you can sit and watch the canal activities. There's also a tourist information point, details of the canal's history and a shop selling canal paraphernalia and souvenirs in the converted warehouse and mill. Continue past the pub along the towpath for a good view of Moss Hall, an old half-timbered house.

Wrenbury

Wrenbury is an old settlement, mentioned in the Domesday book, and much of the village was once owned by the monks of nearby Combermere Abbey. The village remained isolated until the canal and then the railway were built.

St Margaret's church, Wrenbury

Another sandstone church, this time dating from the 16th century, with a late 1700s musicians' gallery and a three-decker Georgian pulpit.

Llangollen Canal

The Ellesmere and Chester Canal, later known as the Llangollen Canal, was completed in 1796 and linked villages such as Wrenbury to the rest of the country, encouraging local industries. The commercial centre was at the lift bridge; the canal warehouse, once used for cheese and dairy products, is now a leisure boat marina. The Dusty Miller pub was a water mill in Victorian times.

Obelisk

The tall obelisk that you may have noticed on the skyline when approaching Marbury commemorates Lord Combermere (formerly Sir Stapleton Cotton), who died in 1865. He led a distinguished military career which resulted in him being created a viscount. The monument is on a hill in Combermere Park, which is not open to the public.

Marbury

Marbury consists of a pretty cluster of half-timbered cottages around a church above the mere. The sycamore tree on the green by the Swan Inn was planted in 1814 to celebrate Wellington's victory over Soult during the Peninsular Wars and is still growing strongly despite

Shropshire Union Canal
at Audlem

a good view of Big Mere from here.

Food and drink
Pubs along the route.
Audlem
(early closing Wednesday).
Wrenbury.

Cycle spares/repairs
None on route.

Campsites
None on route.
See Stage 16.

Nearest railway station
Wrenbury (Shrewsbury - Crewe line).

having been damaged by lightning.

St Michael's church, Marbury

Although the church was first mentioned in 1299, the present building is mostly 15th century and apparently suffering from subsidence. It contains a rare medieval wooden pulpit, the second oldest in Cheshire. There's

Left: Cheshire railings, with every fifth vertical painted black

Below: Malpas

This section takes you to Malpas, a small country town strangely isolated from the main road system, with only B roads leading to it. Malpas stands on a hill, crowned by the squat church of St Oswald, and you continue to cycle uphill when leaving the town on the old Roman road. This doesn't last for long though and it's a steady downhill run on a broad, well-surfaced road to Tilston and quiet lanes beyond, with substantial houses, some old, some new, giving an air of prosperity to the area. Finally the base of the shallow valley of Carden Brook is reached, where old Stretton Mill is sited. Of course, you eventually have to climb out of the valley, but not until you've looped back to Tilston.

Tourist information
Nantwich TIC, Church House, Church Walk, Nantwich, Cheshire CW5 5RG, tel: 01270 610983/610880.
Chester TIC, Town Hall, Northgate St, Chester, Cheshire CH1 2HJ, tel: 01244 317962 or 318356.
Cholmondeley Castle, Malpas, Cheshire, tel: 01829 720383.

Stretton Watermill details from Cheshire Museums, 162 London Rd, Northwich, Cheshire CW9 8AB, tel: 01606 41331.

Cholmondeley Castle (gardens open to public, admission charge)
The unusual name is pronounced 'chumley' and is derived from the original placename, Calmunds Lea. The existing building is relatively modern, built in the early 1800s, but the site is old, being occupied for 800 years by the family. At the time that the castle was built, the old village cottages were demolished and rebuilt on the edge of the park. There's an old-fashioned country grocery store opposite the entrance to the gardens.

Malpas
Malpas, in a strong position on its 400ft (122m) hill, was once an extremely important stronghold, but its castle has long disappeared. However the motte, which is thought to date from the 11th century, is visible on the far side of the churchyard fence, to the rear of the

church. Find the church by turning left in the centre, up a steep hill, past various shops, a pub and half-timbered houses. The window display of the ironmongers and saddlers provides an interesting distraction.

St Oswald's church, Malpas
Although the gates are 18th century, most of the building is 14th century. This church also has a porch with two storeys; the upper storey once housed a priest.

Tilston
This village dates back to Saxon times and surprisingly once had four inns. The old smithy once stood where the Fox & Hounds car park is today.

Stretton Watermill (admission charge)
This lovely old timber-framed building, with wooden weatherboarding, contains 18th century wooden machinery, which has been restored to working order for demonstrations. The mill has two wheels, one on the outside and a later addition housed within a stone extension inside. Wherever water comes into contact with the building, it is made of stone. This mill was part of the Carden estate, where prosperity is much in evidence today, if the substantial mansions are anything to go by.

Food and drink
Pubs along the route.
Shop in No Mans Heath.
Malpas (early closing Wednesday).

Campsites
300yds off-route: Turn right onto A41 to pub on the left. Wheatsheaf Inn, No Mans Heath, Malpas SW14 8DY, tel: 01948 85337. WCs, washbasins (hot water) in the pub, available out of pub hours.

Cycle spares/repairs
None on route.

Cycle hire
South Cheshire Cycle Hire, Meadow View Farm, Crewe Lane South, Farndon, Cheshire, tel: 01829 271242.

Nearest railway station
Whitchurch (Shrewsbury - Crewe line).

Left:
Peckforton *(Stage 17)*

Below:
Shropshire Union Canal near the Shady Oak *(Stage 17)*

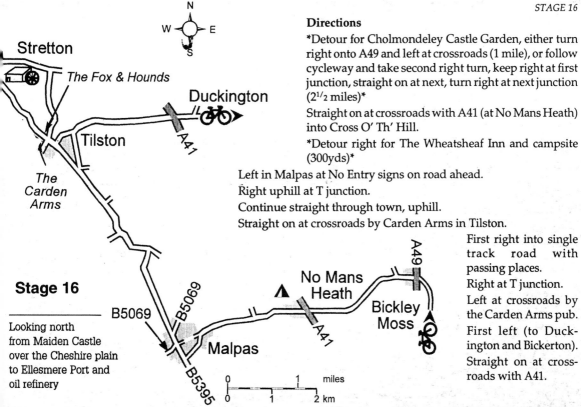

Directions

Detour for Cholmondeley Castle Garden, either turn right onto A49 and left at crossroads (1 mile), or follow cycleway and take second right turn, keep right at first junction, straight on at next, turn right at next junction (2½ miles)

Straight on at crossroads with A41 (at No Mans Heath) into Cross O' Th' Hill.

Detour right for The Wheatsheaf Inn and campsite (300yds)

Left in Malpas at No Entry signs on road ahead.

Right uphill at T junction.

Continue straight through town, uphill.

Straight on at crossroads by Carden Arms in Tilston.

First right into single track road with passing places.

Right at T junction.

Left at crossroads by the Carden Arms pub.

First left (to Duckington and Bickerton).

Straight on at crossroads with A41.

Stage 16

———————

Looking north from Maiden Castle over the Cheshire plain to Ellesmere Port and oil refinery

Stretton

The Fox & Hounds

Duckington

Tilston

The Carden Arms

No Mans Heath

Bickley Moss

B5069

B5069

B5395

Malpas

A41

A49

0   1   miles
0   1   2 km

Duckington to Hargrave (10½ miles)

Now in the sandstone hills, the route follows narrow winding lanes uphill around Larkton Hill, before a climb up to the blind brow of the A534. You need all your senses here to join the main road safely, but the downhill whizz is wonderful, and it seems a shame to break the speed to turn off after such a short run.

The cycleway then passes chocolate-box cottages, some of which are genuinely old, others mock, and the curious Elephant and Castle, before crossing the canal over a viciously steep bridge on a sharp bend, hidden from view until the last minute. Once over the canal, be sure to look back for a grand view of the castles and ridge. Then carry on along the lanes, which eventually bring you back to the canal again.

Tourist information

Nantwich TIC, Church House, Church Walk, Nantwich, Cheshire CW5 5RG, tel: 01270 610983/610880.

Chester TIC, Town Hall, Northgate St, Chester, Cheshire CH1 2HJ, tel: 01244 317962 or 318356.

Peckforton Castle, Stone House Lane, Peckforton, Cheshire, tel: 01829 260930.

Beeston Castle, Beeston, Cheshire, tel: 01829 260464 (summer), 01912 611585 (winter).

Larkton Hill (National Trust, free admission)

Larkton Hill is at the southernmost end of the sandstone ridge which outcrops in central Cheshire. The potential of this vantage point was not lost on our ancestors and it's well worth the walk (no cycling here), from the small car park opposite Pool Farm in Bickerton, to view Maiden Castle. Follow a track and then a path to the top of the hill, then walk left along the edge. You're not looking for a ruin though, but prehistoric earthworks, one of a network along or near this ridge. It's thought that this hill fort (a defended settlement) was constructed in the 1st century BC, which predates the Roman Iron Age. The western side drops away to give uninterrupted views to the west, and defences of double ramparts have been built along the other sides. The remains of earthworks are visible - a shadow of their former selves, estimated to have been at least 20ft wide and 10ft high.

Directions

Straight on at crossroads with A41.

Right at fork.

Straight on at crossroads.

Detour left for campsite (1½ miles)

Straight on at crossroads after Bickerton into Brunty Bank.

Right onto main road (A534).

Left (signposted Beeston Castle) opposite Bickerton Poacher pub.

Cycle through Peckforton to Beeston.

Left at T junction.

Immediately right.

Take second right after Beeston Castle entrance.

Left at T junction after canal.

Detour right to campsite (2½ miles)

First left in Huxley, by the Methodist Jubilee chapel.

Right at T junction.

Stage 17

83 Duckington

They were laced with timber for strength and had stone revetments, enclosing an area of 6300 sq yds (5260 sq m). Although the site hasn't been excavated, it's likely that the area contained clusters of small round huts, pens, granaries and other areas for social, ritual and industrial activities. The fort was destroyed by fire, which smouldered away in the timber ramparts. Carbon dating puts this event at 4000 BC, but what it can't detect is whether the fire was an extension of a heath fire, or the result of enemy action. Its present-day uneven appearance is due to quarrying in the 17th century.

Bickerton Hill (National Trust, free admission)
This is a Site of Special Scientific Interest because it's one of the few remaining heathlands in Cheshire but it's being invaded by self-sown birch trees, so the National Trust grazes Welsh Black cattle here in the spring months to browse the young trees and prevent seedlings from establishing. The Welsh Black is a hardy breed, used since pre-Roman times on the Welsh hills.

Coppermine Chimney, Gallantry Bank, Bickerton (view from road)
As you whizz down the main road, you may notice an old chimney in the field opposite a lay-by and lane. This is all that is visible of coppermines dating from the late 1600s. The chimney isn't that old, though - it was built along with an engine house in 1856. All the buildings except the chimney were demolished in the 1920s, when the mine was closed and the shafts made safe.

Gallantry Bank
The name is derived from Gallow-Tree Bank, so called because the body of a murderer was gibbeted here in the mid-17th century.

Peckforton Castle (admission charge)
This massive castle was built in 1850 for Sir John Tollemache, in the style of a medieval fortress, at the northern end of Peckforton ridge. It's visible from a distance, but the woodland surrounding it hides it from view from this section of the cycleway. Look back once you reach Beeston village for a view of its turrets and towers above the tree tops.

Peckforton village
The fairy-tale estate cottages of Peckforton are not all that they seem. When Tollemache bought the estate, he introduced some continuity of style by having cast-iron lattice casement windows inserted into existing 17th

Beeston Castle

century black and white cottages, to match his new farmhouses and cottages. He also incorporated timbers in the gable ends of the new buildings and the same window styles, for uniformity.

The design of one of the 17th century cottages, a half-timbered, thatched building on Stone House Lane, nearly opposite Peckforton Hall Lane, is interesting. The design is derived from a longhouse, where animals and humans lived under the same roof and both entered through the same door. This type of dwelling shows the next stage in development, where humans and animals had their own quarters, and entered by separate doors.

The humans' door was on the long side of the house and the animals' door was in the gable end.

Elephant and Castle, Laundry Cottage (private, view from road)

Look out for cottages on the left with a tall holly hedge by the roadside. Once past the hedging, look up the farm drive and you'll see an elephant with a glazed castle on its back, carved around 1859 by a local stonemason, Mr Watson, who was working on Peckforton Castle at the time. He used stone from the same quarry as the castle and set up the statue in his cottage garden. When the cottage was demolished, the carving was moved to this site. The choice of subject may be connected with the Corbett family arms, which features an elephant. This family owned Peckforton up to around 1626.

Beeston Castle (English Heritage, admission charge)

The castle stands invincible on its rocky outcrop, which was fortified in the bronze age. The castle ruin that you see now dates from the early 1200s and formed part of the Welsh border defences. It became redundant once hostilities ceased and fell into disrepair, only to become important again during the Civil War, which caused its partial destruction. It's still worth a visit for the views from its walls, but make sure it's a fine day to make the most of such a steep walk uphill.

The turreted entrance by the roadside was built in the 19th century for Lord Tollemache to complement other buildings on his estate. The entrance now houses a small exhibition for visitors to the castle. There's also a WC available during opening hours only (free for castle visitors, 10p for passers-by).

Food and drink

Pubs along the route.

Catering van on Beeston picnic site during busy periods.

Campsites

1½ miles off-route: After turning left at crossroads, continue to A534, turn right, pub on right.

The Durham Heifer, Nantwich Rd, Broxton, Chester CH3 9JH, tel: 01829 782253.

Facilities in pub, only available during opening hours.

2½ miles off-route: After turning right at T junction, turn first left, continue straight on to Tarporley village, look for campsite on far side of village, on the left.

Brickfield Farm, 2 High St, Tarporley, Cheshire, tel: 01829 732738. WC.

Cycle spares/repairs
None on route.

Nearest railway station
Chester (Chester - Manchester line).

*Elephant and Castle in
Laundry Cottage's
garden, Peckforton*

You really are on the Cheshire plain now. It's level pedalling alongside the canal, where the long line of moored boats of all types, styles, colours and names add interest. Christleton is a pretty little village complete with smithy, tiny village green, pump, wooden shelter, and further on, a pool inhabited by ducks and swans, overlooked by almshouses. It's quite a shock to emerge from these quiet villages and lanes to cross over the busy A55 which rings southern Chester. It's not much further before the route merges with the busy roads on the outskirts of the city, fortunately making use of new cycletracks on the busiest sections.

Tourist information
Chester TIC, Town Hall, Northgate St, Chester, Cheshire CH1 2HJ, tel: 01244 317962 or 318356.

Hockenhull Platts
The wide and quiet country lane which degenerates into a track and then a public footpath (no cycling here) was once the main Chester to London road. Venture along the cobbled footpath past the coppice and you'll come to three packhorse bridges over the River Gowy and the surrounding wet areas. These bridges date from medieval times and there's a record of the Black Prince granting 20 shillings for repairs to the bridge in 1353, presumably after passing this way on his state visit from Staffordshire. There was a petition made for a collection to cover repairs made in 1614 and further work was necessary in the 18th century, which is what you can see now. By the mid-17th century, there were alternative routes to the north and south which were used by wheeled traffic. Fortunately proposals to put a new road through here never came about. Now the wildlife and the occasional walker have this once busy thoroughfare to themselves.

Food and drink
Waverton - shops opposite Brownheath Rd.
Christleton.
Chester, at junction of A51 with Green Lane and further along Green Lane (shops may observe early closing Wednesday).

Stage 18

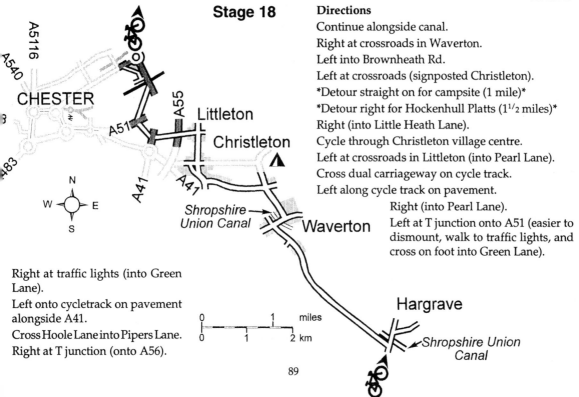

Directions

Continue alongside canal.

Right at crossroads in Waverton.

Left into Brownheath Rd.

Left at crossroads (signposted Christleton).

Detour straight on for campsite (1 mile)

Detour right for Hockenhull Platts (1½ miles)

Right (into Little Heath Lane).

Cycle through Christleton village centre.

Left at crossroads in Littleton (into Pearl Lane).

Cross dual carriageway on cycle track.

Left along cycle track on pavement.

Right (into Pearl Lane).

Left at T junction onto A51 (easier to dismount, walk to traffic lights, and cross on foot into Green Lane).

Right at traffic lights (into Green Lane).

Left onto cycletrack on pavement alongside A41.

Cross Hoole Lane into Pipers Lane.

Right at T junction (onto A56).

89

Campsites

1 mile off-route: Continue along lane. Look for farm on right-hand side.

Birch Bank Farm, Stamford Lane, Christleton, Chester CH3 7QD, tel: 01244 335233. WCs, hot showers.

Cycle spares/repairs

The Cycle Centre, 19 Charles St, Hoole, Chester, Cheshire, tel: 01244 340420.

Davies Bros (Cycles) Ltd, 6-8 Cuppin St, Chester, Cheshire, tel: 01244 319204/318899.

Dave Miller Cycles, 41 Frodsham St, Chester, Cheshire, tel: 01244 326506.

Cycle hire

Davies Brothers (Cycles) Ltd - see above.

Nearest railway station

Chester (Chester - Manchester line).

Useful addresses and phone numbers

Cheshire cycling information

Cycling Officer, Cheshire County Council, Goldsmith House, Hamilton Place, Chester CH1 1SE, tel: 01244 603617.

Heritage and Recreation, Cheshire County Council, Goldsmith House, Hamilton Place, Chester CH1 1SE, tel: 01244 602843.

The Secretary, Cyclists' Touring Club (Chester and North Wales District Association), Golborne Bridge, Handley, Chester SH3 9DR, tel: 01829 70224.

British Rail, Manchester, tel: 0161 832 8353.

National cycling information

Cyclists' Touring Club, Cotterell House, 69 Meadrow, Godalming, Surrey GU7 3HS, tel: 01483 417217.

Sustrans, 35 King St, Bristol BS1 4DZ, tel: 01179 268893.

Campsites

Camping & Caravanning Club Ltd, Greenfields House, Westwood Way, Coventry CV4 8JH, tel: 01203 694995.

Places of interest

Cheshire Wildlife Trust (nature reserves), Grebe House, Reaseheath, Nantwich, Cheshire CW5 6DA, tel: 01270 610180.

National Gardens Scheme (private gardens open to the public on occasional days), Hatchlands Park, East Clandon, Guildford, Surrey GU4 7RT, tel: 01483 211535.

The National Trust (houses, gardens and open countryside), 36 Queen Anne's Gate, London SW1H 9AS, tel: 0171 222 9251.

Cycle bags

Carradice of Nelson Ltd, Westmoreland Works, St Mary's St, Nelson BB9 7BA, tel: 01282 615886.

Field & Trek plc (mail order), 3 Wates Way, Brentwood, Essex CM15 9TB, tel: 01277 233122.

Karrimor International Ltd, Petre Rd, Clayton-le-Moors, Accrington, Lancs BB5 5JZ, tel: 01254 385911.

Ortlieb from Lyon Equipment, Dent, Sedbergh, Cumbria LA10 5QL, tel: 01539 625493.

VauDe (UK), Unit DC 72/5, Haltwhistle Ind Est, Haltwhistle, Northumberland NE49 9HA, tel: 01434 320744.

Jack Wolfskin Adventure Equipment, 12A Kingstown Broadway, Carlisle, Cumbria CA3 0HA, tel: 01228 27624.

Cycle rucksacks

Berghaus Ltd, 17-19 Brindley Rd, Hertburn Ind Est, District 11, Washington, Tyne & Wear NE37 2SF, tel: 0191 415 0200.

Karrimor - see above.

Cycle clothing

Berghaus - see above.

Karrimor - see above.

Regatta from Risol Ltd, Risol House, Mercury Way, Urmston, Manchester M41 9RR, tel: 0161 747 2971.

Ronhill Sports Ltd, Dawson St, Hyde, Cheshire SK14 1RD, tel: 0161 366 5020.

CICERONE GUIDES

Cicerone publish a wide range of reliable guides to walking, climbing, cycling and related outdoor topics

LAKE DISTRICT - General Books
CONISTON COPPER A History
CHRONICLES OF MILNTHORPE
A DREAM OF EDEN -LAKELAND DALES
EDEN TAPESTRY
THE HIGH FELLS OF LAKELAND
KENDAL - A SOCIAL HISTORY
LAKELAND - A taste to remember (Recipes)
LAKELAND VILLAGES
LAKELAND TOWNS
LAKELAND PANORAMAS
THE LAKERS
THE LOST RESORT? (Morecambe)
LOST LANCASHIRE (Furness area)
THE PRIORY OF CARTMEL
REFLECTIONS ON THE LAKES
AN ILLUSTRATED COMPANION INTO LAKELAND

LAKE DISTRICT - Guide Books
THE BORDERS OF LAKELAND
BIRDS OF MORECAMBE BAY
CASTLES IN CUMBRIA
CONISTON COPPER MINES Field Guide
THE CUMBRIA CYCLE WAY
THE EDEN WAY
IN SEARCH OF WESTMORLAND
SHORT WALKS IN LAKELAND-1: SOUTH LAKELAND
SCRAMBLES IN THE LAKE DISTRICT

THE TARNS OF LAKELAND
WALKING ROUND THE LAKES
WALKS IN SILVERDALE/ARNSIDE
WESTMORLAND HERITAGE WALK
WINTER CLIMBS IN THE LAKE DISTRICT

NORTHERN ENGLAND (outside the Lakes
BIRDWATCHING ON MERSEYSIDE
CANAL WALKS Vol 1 North
CANOEISTS GUIDE TO THE NORTH EAST
THE CLEVELAND WAY & MISSING LINK
THE DALES WAY
DOUGLAS VALLEY WAY
WALKING IN THE FOREST OF BOWLAND
HADRIANS WALL Vol 1 The Wall Walk
HERITAGE TRAILS IN NW ENGLAND
THE ISLE OF MAN COASTAL PATH
IVORY TOWERS & DRESSED STONES (Follies)
THE LANCASTER CANAL
LANCASTER CANAL WALKS
A WALKERS GUIDE TO THE LANCASTER CANAL
LAUGHS ALONG THE PENNINE WAY
A NORTHERN COAST-TO-COAST
NORTH YORK MOORS Walks
THE REIVERS WAY (Northumberland)
THE RIBBLE WAY
ROCK CLIMBS LANCASHIRE & NW
WALKING DOWN THE LUNE
WALKING IN THE SOUTH PENNINES
WALKING IN THE NORTH PENNINES
WALKING IN THE WOLDS
WALKS IN THE YORKSHIRE DALES (3 VOL)
WALKS IN LANCASHIRE WITCH COUNTRY
WALKS IN THE NORTH YORK MOORS (2 VOL)
WALKS TO YORKSHIRE WATERFALLS (3 vol)
WALKS ON THE WEST PENNINE MOORS

WALKING NORTHERN RAILWAYS (2 vol)
THE YORKSHIRE DALES A walker's guide

DERBYSHIRE & EAST MIDLANDS
KINDER LOG
HIGH PEAK WALKS
WHITE PEAK WAY
WHITE PEAK WALKS - 2 Vols
WEEKEND WALKS IN THE PEAK DISTRICT
THE VIKING WAY
THE DEVIL'S MILL / WHISTLING CLOUGH (Novels)

WALES & WEST MIDLANDS
ASCENT OF SNOWDON
WALKING IN CHESHIRE
CLWYD ROCK
HEREFORD & THE WYE VALLEY A Walker's Guide
HILLWALKING IN SNOWDONIA
HILL WALKING IN WALES (2 Vols)
MOUNTAINS OF ENGLAND & WALES Vol 1WALES
WALKING OFFA'S DYKE PATH
THE RIDGES OF SNOWDONIA
ROCK CLIMBS IN WEST MIDLANDS
SARN HELEN Walking Roman Road
SCRAMBLES IN SNOWDONIA
SEVERN WALKS
THE SHROPSHIRE HILLS A Walker's Guide
SNOWDONIA WHITE WATER SEA & SURF
WALKING DOWN THE WYE
WELSH WINTER CLIMBS

SOUTH & SOUTH WEST ENGLAND
WALKING IN THE CHILTERNS
COTSWOLD WAY
COTSWOLD WALKS (3 VOLS)
WALKING ON DARTMOOR
WALKERS GUIDE TO DARTMOOR PUBS
WALKING IN DORSET

EXMOOR & THE QUANTOCKS
THE KENNET & AVON WALK
LONDON THEME WALKS
AN OXBRIDGE WALK
A SOUTHERN COUNTIES BIKE GUIDE
THE SOUTHERN-COAST-TO-COAST
SOUTH DOWNS WAY & DOWNS LINK
SOUTH WEST WAY - 2 Vol
THE TWO MOORS WAY Dartmoor-Exmoor
WALKS IN KENT Bk 2
THE WEALDWAY & VANGUARD WAY

SCOTLAND
THE BORDER COUNTRY - WALKERS GUIDE
BORDER PUBS & INNS A Walker's Guide
CAIRNGORMS WINTER CLIMBS
WALKING THE GALLOWAY HILLS
THE ISLAND OF RHUM
THE SCOTTISH GLENS (Mountainbike Guides)
    4 volumes
SCOTTISH RAILWAY WALKS
SCRAMBLES IN LOCHABER
SCRAMBLES IN SKYE
SKI TOURING IN SCOTLAND
TORRIDON A Walker's Guide
WALKS from the WEST HIGHLAND RAILWAY
WINTER CLIMBS BEN NEVIS & GLENCOE

REGIONAL BOOKS UK & IRELAND
THE ALTERNATIVE PENNINE WAY
CANAL WALKS Vol.1: North
LIMESTONE - 100 BEST CLIMBS
THE PACKHORSE BRIDGES OF ENGLAND
THE RELATIVE HILLS OF BRITAIN
THE MOUNTAINS OF ENGLAND & WALES
    VOL 1 WALES, VOL 2 ENGLAND
THE MOUNTAINS OF IRELAND

CICERONE GUIDES

Cicerone publish a wide range of reliable guides to walking and climbing abroad

FRANCE, BELGIUM & LUXEMBOURG
THE BRITTANY COASTAL PATH
CHAMONIX MONT BLANC - A Walking Guide
THE CORSICAN HIGH LEVEL ROUTE: GR20
FRENCH ROCK
THE PYRENEAN TRAIL: GR10
THE RLS (Stevenson) TRAIL
ROCK CLIMBS IN BELGIUM & LUXEMBOURG
ROCK CLIMBS IN THE VERDON
TOUR OF MONT BLANC
TOUR OF THE OISANS: GR54
TOUR OF THE QUEYRAS
WALKING THE FRENCH ALPS: GR5
WALKING THE FRENCH GORGES (Provence)
WALKING IN HAUTE SAVOIE
WALKS IN VOLCANO COUNTRY (Auvergne)
THE WAY OF ST JAMES: GR65

FRANCE / SPAIN
WALKS AND CLIMBS IN THE PYRENEES
ROCK CLIMBS IN THE PYRENEES

SPAIN & PORTUGAL
ANDALUSIAN ROCK CLIMBS
BIRDWATCHING IN MALLORCA
COSTA BLANCA CLIMBS
MOUNTAIN WALKS ON THE COSTA
BLANCAMOUNTAINS OF CENTRAL SPAIN
WALKING IN MALLORCA
WALKS & CLIMBS IN THE PICOS DE EUROPA

THE WAY OF ST JAMES: SPAIN
WALKING IN THE ALGARVE

FRANCE / SWITZERLAND
CHAMONIX TO ZERMATT
The Walker's Haute Route
THE JURA - Walking the High Route
and Winter Ski Traverses

SWITZERLAND
THE ALPINE PASS ROUTE
THE BERNESE ALPS
CENTRAL SWITZERLAND
THE GRAND TOUR OF MONTE ROSA (inc Italy)
WALKS IN THE ENGADINE
WALKING IN TICINO
THE VALAIS - A Walking Guide

GERMANY / AUSTRIA / EASTERN EUROPE
HUT-TO-HUT IN THE STUBAI ALPS
THE HIGH TATRAS
THE KALKALPEN TRAVERSE
KING LUDWIG WAY
KLETTERSTEIG - Scrambles
MOUNTAIN WALKING IN AUSTRIA

ITALY & SLOVENIA
ALTA VIA - High Level Walks in the Dolomites
CENTRAL ITALIAN ALPS
CLASSIC CLIMBS IN THE DOLOMITES
THE GRAND TOUR OF MONTE ROSA inc Switzerland))
ITALIAN ROCK - Rock Climbs in Northern Italy
VIA FERRATA - Scrambles in the Dolomites
WALKING IN THE DOLOMITES

WALKS IN THE JULIAN ALPS

MEDITERRANEAN COUNTRIES
THE ATLAS MOUNTAINS
CRETE: Off the beaten track
WALKING IN CYPRUS
THE MOUNTAINS OF GREECE
THE MOUNTAINS OF TURKEY
TREKS & CLIMBS IN WADI RUM, JORDAN
THE ALA DAG - Climbs & Treks (Turkey)

OTHER COUNTRIES
ADVENTURE TREKS - W. N. AMERICA
ANNAPURNA TREKKERS GUIDE
EVEREST - A TREKKERS GUIDE
CLASSIC TRAMPS IN NEW ZEALAND
LANGTANG - A Trekkers Guide
MOUNTAIN WALKING IN AFRICA 1: KENYA
ROCK CLIMBS IN HONG KONG
TREKKING IN THE CAUCAUSUS
TREKKING IN NEPAL
TREKKING - WESTERN NORTH AMERICA

GENERAL OUTDOOR BOOKS
THE ADVENTURE ALTERNATIVE
FAMILY CAMPING
FIRST AID FOR HILLWALKERS
THE HILL WALKERS MANUAL
LIMESTONE -100 BEST CLIMBS IN BRITAIN
MOUNTAIN WEATHER
MOUNTAINEERING LITERATURE
MODERN ALPINE CLIMBING
MODERN SNOW & ICE TECHNIQUES
ROPE TECHNIQUES IN MOUNTAINEERING

CANOEING
CANOEIST'S GUIDE TO THE NORTH EAST
SNOWDONIA WILD WATER, SEA & SURF
WILDWATER CANOEING

CARTOON BOOKS
ON FOOT & FINGER
ON MORE FEET & FINGERS
LAUGHS ALONG THE PENNINE WAY
THE WALKERS

Also a full range of guidebooks to walking, scrambling, ice-climbing, rock climbing, and other adventurous pursuits in Britain and abroad

---

Other guides are constantly being added to the Cicerone List. Available from bookshops, outdoor equipment shops or direct (send s.a.e. for price list) from CICERONE, 2 POLICE SQUARE, MILNTHORPE, CUMBRIA, LA7 7PY